CONTENTS

NARMADA
MADHYA PRADESH
INDORE
Julwania
NH 3
Sendhwa
TAPTI
130
DELHI
Agra
INDIA
Khajuraho
Sanchi
Bodh Gaya
Ajanta
Bhimbetka
KOLKATA
Ellora
MUMBAI
Konarak
Pattadakal
Old Goa
Hampi
BANGALORE
CHENNAI
Mamallapuram
Lakshadweep
Thanjavur
Andaman & Nicobar Islands
Bhusawal
Edalabad
53
93
57
Jalgaon
Dhule
NH 6
Malkapur
NAGPUR
GIRNA
Girna Dam
55
93
66
AJANTA
Fardapur
Buldana
Chalisgaon
101
Chikhli
Pitalkhora
Sillod
62
PURNA
80
ELLORA
66
Khuldabad
27
Lonar
Daulatabad
Aurangabad
Lonar Meteorite Crater
60
Jalna
GODAVARI
48
Mantha
SHTRA
Paithan
101
NANDED
Shevgaon
87
85
Pathri
Ahmadnagar
Bid
74
66
Jamkhed
98
NOT TO SCALE
LEGEND
AJANTA World Heritage Site
Inter-State Boundary
Railway Line
NH 2 National Highway
Other Roads
Airport

GOOD EARTH

FROM AJANTA TO ELLORA

TRAVEL GUIDE

EICHER GOODEARTH LIMITED
New Delhi

Supported by
Incredible India
Ministry of Tourism, Government of India

A GOOD EARTH PUBLICATION

ISBN 81-87780-29-0

Editor and Publisher: Swati Mitra

Design : Anjan Chakravorty
Research & Editing : Samia Sharma, Parvati Sharma
Editorial Assistance : Bidisha Ganguly
Photographs : Arindam Sen Gupta
The photographs on the following pages have been reproduced with kind permission of Archaeological Survey of India:
pp. 19, 20, 36, 38, 44, 48, 72, 82, 84
Photograph on p. 9 is reproduced from H Cousens, *Architectural Antiquities of Western India* (London, 1926).

Great care has been taken in the compilation, updation and validation of information, and every effort has been made to ensure that all information is as up-to-date as possible at the time of going to press. Details like telephone and fax numbers, opening hours and travel information may change. However, the Publishers are not responsible for errors, if any, and their consequences.

The Publishers would be happy to receive suggestions and corrections for inclusion in the next edition.
Please write to Executive Publisher, Eicher Goodearth Ltd, Eicher House, 12 Commercial Complex, Greater Kailash II (Masjid Moth), New Delhi 110 048.

This publication has been supported by
Ministry of Tourism, Government of India

Printed by Brijbasi Art Press Ltd, New Delhi
on behalf of Eicher Goodearth Ltd.

GOD AND THE ARTIST:

THE RELIGIOUS EXCAVATIONS OF AJANTA AND ELLORA

Beginning two centuries before the birth of Christ, sculptors, masons, artists and monks gave over their lives to excavating the volcanic hills of what would later become the state of Maharashtra in India. The most beautiful and spectacular results of their dedication are the rock-cut temples of Ajanta and Ellora.

Buddhist, Hindu and Jaina philosophies guided their labours, and the legends and canonical precepts of each religion gave to the paintings and sculptures in these caves a contemporary resonance that, even today, continues to shape Indian art.

***Apsara*, Cave 17**

The Geography of the Region

Some 65 million years ago, when our continents were not yet formed as we know them, a spectacular volcanic explosion freed the Indian subcontinent to drift north to its current location. That explosion also released enough lava to cover approximately 1.5 million sq kms.

As the lava cooled, it was transformed into basalt – an igneous rock that is somewhat porous and softer in comparison to other, non-volcanic varieties. Today the remnants of that explosion are basalt deposits 2,000 m thick, covering an area of 500,000 sq kms

in west-central India, known as the Deccan Trap.

It is unclear how the first excavators realised that the hillsides of the Deccan were uniquely suited to carving and it became a centre of astounding rock-cut architecture: most impressive being the Ajanta and Ellora caves.

The region itself has been inhabited for 20,000 years; Upper Palaeolithic, Mesolithic and Chalcolithic remains have been found here. In these terms, the Ajanta caves are very recent – they have been dated to between the 2nd century BC and the 7th century AD. The Ellora excavations happened even later, between the 5th and 12th centuries AD.

A panoramic view of the Ajanta Caves

The History of the Excavations

Why, in those ancient times, did monks and architects, artists and masons dedicate their lives to carving monuments to their religions from stone?

Written records are rare. One of the earliest testimonies to Ajanta, for example, is based on hearsay: the 7th century Chinese traveller Hiuen-Tsang mentions a 'monastery in a deep defile', without actually having seen it.

It is speculated that the monks of the Deccan may have realised what *could* be done with rock because of Emperor Ashoka's attempts at excavating the Barabar and Nagarjuni Hills in Bihar.

The Ajanta caves offer a clue as to why they thought it *should* be done. An inscription in Cave 26 says that it is good to 'set up monuments on mountains that will endure as long as the moon and the sun continue, for a man will exist to enjoy paradise as long as his memory is green on earth'.

Perhaps, also, it was fortunate that they stumbled upon hillsides amenable to carving when the steadily expanding monastic orders needed shelter during the monsoon months.

Another factor, however, was needed to give the excavations a thrust – patronage. There are hundreds of rock-cut excavations in Maharashtra, extremely elaborate and completed with seemingly superhuman effort. Where did the wealth that allowed this effort come from?

Photograph of Cave 26, taken in 1880

Buddha's meditation continues uninterrupted despite the Temptation of Mara, Cave 26

Merchants were probably the most readily available source of funds. At Ajanta, Cave 12 is attributed to a trader from Thana named Ghanamadada; and Cave 2 bears an inscription that reads: 'Why should not a temple be raised by those possessing wealth and desirous of mundane happiness as also of liberation, for happiness of the world as also for their own final emancipation?'

Commercial centres like Sopara, then the biggest port on the Arabian Sea, or Paithan, which exported perfume to countries like Egypt, generated great wealth for their inhabitants, many of whom chose to donate some of their profit to their religion.

Paithan is also thought to have been the capital of the Satavahanas. It is speculated that this dynasty ruled the Deccan for about 300 years, contributing greatly to the region's political stability and creating an environment in which trade, art and religion could be freely practised.

Numerous sculpted images of Buddha covering the façade of Cave 19

Many of the early excavations in the Deccan were begun under the Satavahanas. Some of the caves at Nasik are engraved with references to the dynasty. These and the early Ajanta caves (8, 9, 10, 12, 13 and 15A), those at Bhaja, Pitalkhora and Karle are dated to between 200 BC and 200 AD, which are approximately the dates of Satavahana dominance in the Deccan.

Painting at the entrance to Cave 17. The top panel depicts past Buddhas along with Maitreya, the Future Buddha

Increasingly, the connection between trade and excavations became very intimate. In fact, because archaeologists knew of an ancient trade route from the port of Chaul (about 15 kms from Alibag, and later a Portuguese settlement) to the state's interior, they were convinced there *must* be caves nearby too. And, indeed, they did find some caves of the Hinayana period near the town.

Ajanta

The Discovery

The story of Ajanta's 'discovery' is far better documented than that of its creation. Soot deposits on the cave walls indicate that even when they fell into oblivion, nomadic or tribal communities may have used them for shelter. No written records, however, and no pilgrimages recalled their existence; and it was a hunting expedition led by the British captain John Smith, from the Madras Army, that accidentally stumbled on them in 1819. They were named after a small village nearby.

Naturally, there followed a great flurry of archaeological and documentation activity, led by James Fergusson who presented the first academic paper on Ajanta to the Royal Asiatic Society in 1843. He argued that the caves be preserved, and some record made of the paintings within.

It is fortunate that his arguments were convincing. In the years between their discovery and the first attempts at preservation, the caves were subject to increasing vandalism. A certain petty official had even gifted away pieces of sculpture – a group of five male heads eventually found its way to an auction at Sotheby's!

Two extensive projects to copy the paintings began one after the other. An army officer, Captain Robert Gill, spent over 20 years making meticulous reproductions – most of which were destroyed in a fire. Another project initiated at the cost of Rs 50,000, was led by John Griffiths, head of the JJ School of Art at

Bombay. Many of Griffiths' reproductions were also published and became available to artists and art historians around the world.

This was the second time the paintings of Ajanta had an international audience.

Bodhisattva Vajrapani, Cave 1

The History

The Ajanta excavations were begun under the Satavahanas. Although they were not particularly active patrons of Buddhism, the merchants who prospered under their rule were – and donated generously to the artists and monks in the caves.

With the decline of the Satavahanas, work at Ajanta stopped. There is little more than speculative evidence to connect the two events; however, the Deccan witnessed a great deal of conflict in the next three to four centuries, which cannot have been conducive to artistic activity. Perhaps, too, the trade route along which Ajanta was situated fell into disuse, and

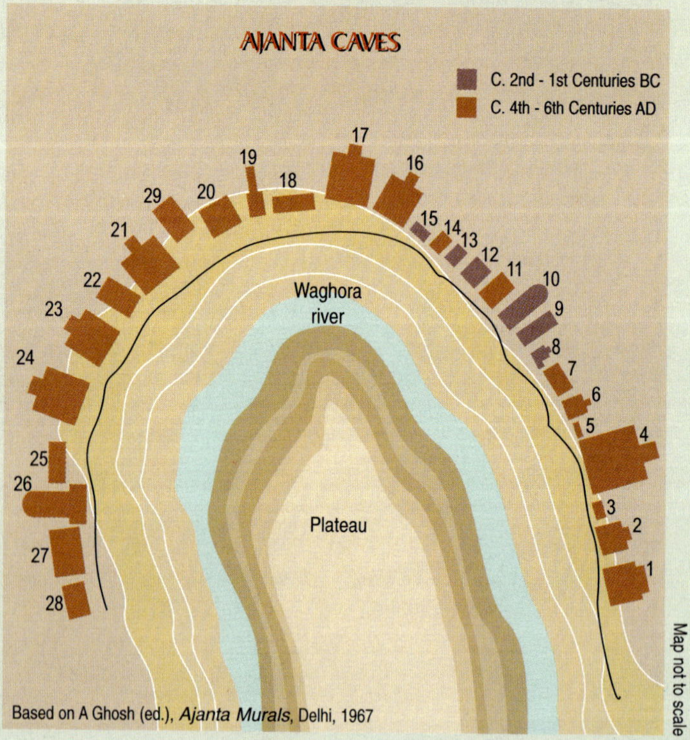

Entrance, Cave 26

the caves were abandoned because monks, being entirely dependent on alms, could not afford to live in complete isolation.

Eventually, with the rise of the Vakatakas, stability returned to the region. This dynasty ruled from the 5th to 7th centuries AD, and was allied to the great Gupta Empire in northern India. Once again, a prosperous trading community could afford to donate to religion. The Vakatakas' own link with Buddhism was an additional boost – Ajanta's Cave 16 is a generous gift from Varahadeva, King Harishena's minister.

Contact with the Guptas meant that the monks and artists of Ajanta learnt of the philosophies and aesthetics current in the subcontinent's other Buddhist centres such as Sarnath, Bodh Gaya and Mathura. The last had a very strong influence on Ajanta's sculpture.

The Paintings

There is a great power in the art of these caves which, according to Ingrid Aall, 'lie like a string of pearls around the waist of the mountain'. As their fame spread, the paintings at Ajanta inspired mural art in regions as diverse as Sri Lanka, Afghanistan and China.

However, because the caves were excavated over many centuries, they were subject to many variations of style and technique. Although excavations were always either *chaityas* (sanctuaries) or *viharas* (monasteries), their diverse aesthetic styles stemmed from changes in the art's philosophical underpinnings.

The early caves are products of Hinayana Buddhism, which believed in symbolic representations of Buddha. Figures of Buddha are therefore significantly absent as the early Buddhists were not allowed to represent the Lord in his bodily form. Of the early caves, 9, 10 and 12 are most interesting, though not much survives of the Hinayana paintings, most of them having been painted over by later artists. However, in Cave 10, traces of earlier paintings are still visible. The figures of Buddha outside Cave 9 are later additions.

A princess, Cave 17

With only six pigments in his hand, the Ajanta artist created the vocabulary of the entire colour range, each speaking its own language and giving meaning to others...

Ingrid Aall

> Art is a collaboration between God and the artist, and the less the artist does the better
>
> **André Gide**

Meanwhile the caves, originally intended as shelters for monks during the monsoon months, became places where pilgrims, merchants and travellers from around the world would converge. The art on their walls was used to spread the message of Buddha. This was done primarily through representations of the *Jataka* tales.

Buddha in two different postures, Cave 2

With time, and as the Mahayana tradition became popular, Buddhist art changed to representing images of Buddha that emphasised his divinity. In this context portrayals of Bodhisattvas became favourite subjects.

Ajanta's artists chose to depict many details of royal, monastic and lay life. Scenes of courtly love are executed with unmatched tenderness. Principal and secondary characters, whether divine, human or animal, are painted in exquisite detail, complete with different hairstyles, dress, accessories and expressions. Men and women with foreign features, dressed in exotic styles reflect the diverse influences on the artists.

In other cases, the murals hint at the continuities in Indian culture through the ages. Cave 16, for example, shows dancers in poses that remain current.

Detail from the panel showing the Conversion of Nanda, Cave 1

The artists reserved their best for women and Buddha. One of Ajanta's most beautiful women is Princess Sundari in Cave 16. She is shown mourning the loss of her husband, Nanda, taken by Buddha to join the Order. Griffiths said of this mural that 'for pathos and sentiment and

the unmistakable way of telling its story this… cannot be surpassed in the history of art'. Indeed, the woebegone princess, half-prone in the arms of her attendants, with eyes barely open, her limbs tired and thin, encapsulates the grief of all lovers when parted from their beloveds.

The Dark Princess of Cave 1 is equally renowned for her grace and delicacy. She is just below Bodhisattva Vajrapani and is one of the most beautiful women in Ajanta. In the same cave, the Bodhisattva Vajrapani wears a gloriously intricate crown and, for sheer power and vitality, is considered one of Ajanta's treasures.

Conceptually, however, each story and every brush stroke attempted to convey the essentially Buddhist notion of the Wheel of Life: of transmigration and the eternal search for freedom from transmigration.

It is also speculated by historians that monks commissioned some of the more repetitive series of Buddha images to buy themselves religious merit. According to M N Deshpande, they were supposed to 'endow the donor with good looks, good luck and good qualities'.

Once a group of six monks had a bold design made with the figures of women, figures of men, in a dwelling place. People who saw the pictures said: 'Like householders who enjoy pleasures of the senses!' This matter was brought to the notice of Buddha, who said: 'Monks, you should not have a bold design made with figures of women, figures of men. I allow monks only wreath-work, creeper work, swordfish teeth, the five strips [of cloth design].

From the *Vinaya* texts

The Sculpture

Ajanta's sculptors were tremendously skilled, capable of moulding rock into the most subtle emotions. Their greatest accomplishment is often considered the giant Parinirvana Buddha in Cave 26. Inspired by the most poignant moment from Buddha's life, it shows him preparing to die and attain liberation from the cycle of death and rebirth. A silent, meditative dignity radiates from the sculpture.

A more playful impulse may have sparked the four deer carved in Cave 1. All four deer share the same head – and what might in other hands have been grotesque, or merely comic, is here almost hypnotisingly intriguing.

Other subjects of sculpture at Ajanta include the Buddha and the Bodhisattvas, *nagas* and *yakshas* and floral and geometric designs. Particularly remarkable are the many Buddha figures carved on the façade of Cave 19.

The Parinirvana Buddha, Cave 26

Technique

There is some confusion about whether Ajanta paintings are frescoes. Derived from the Italian for 'fresh', frescoes are painted on wet plaster so that when they dry, they become part of the surface. In Ajanta, work was done on a base of mud and lime – but only when that base had dried. In that sense, Ajanta's paintings are murals, not frescos.

The artists worked with six colours: red and yellow ochre, black and white, mineral green and blue. The last was made from crushed lapis lazuli and was used with brilliant effect. In Cave 1, for example, a peacock outlined with crushed stone seems to leap out of the walls.

A more perplexing question, for both lay visitors and scholars, is how these ancient artists managed to light the caves enough to do such intricate work. Some speculate that they contrived a solution with oil lamps, others contend that they used water to multiply the light of lamps, or metal mirrors to reflect sunlight indoors. Most intriguing is the theory that they created detailed stencils of the paintings *outdoors* and then replicated them inside.

The art of Ajanta has been subject to more than its fair share of criticism, ranging from early Orientalist theories that argued Ajanta had Greek antecedents to current hypotheses on how Ajanta has influenced much of modern Indian art.

In the end, perhaps no analysis can quite compare with the fact that such a tremendous enterprise was ever contemplated, let alone achieved.

The beautiful consort of Bodhisattva Padmapani, Cave 1

Ellora

By the 7th century AD, religious, commercial and artistic activity around Ajanta began to decline. The last two caves here, 28 and 29, were left incomplete. Concurrently, another trade route connecting ports along the Arabian Sea with cities like Paithan became widely used. It is along this route that the Ellora excavations began.

From the 5th to the 12th centuries AD, Ellora witnessed three strains of art, Buddhist, Hindu and Jaina, each patronised by a succession of royal dynasties.

The Buddhist monuments were probably built during the reign of the Kalachuris of Mahismati and the Chalukyas of Badami who ruled the region briefly before being ousted by the Rashtrakutas.

View of Kailasha temple and the surrounding countryside

The solemn mystery of these great colonnaded caverns, yet orderly and symmetrical in their formation, would appeal to minds imaginative and intensely receptive...

Percy Brown

The Rashtrakutas patronised Hindu architecture, and the Brahmanical excavations at Ellora were made during their rule. An inscription on the back wall of Cave 15 attributes its construction to the king Dantidurga (c. 753-57 AD); and the great Kailasha temple was commissioned by Dantidurga's uncle and successor, Krishna I (c. 757-83 AD).

Excavation of the Jaina group of caves in Ellora began after the decline of the Rashtrakutas, probably under the Kalyani Chalukyas and the Yadavas of Deogiri (later Daulatabad).

For reasons open to debate, Ellora did not share Ajanta's fate. There are many accounts of travellers visiting the site, including those of the Arab geographer Al-Mas'udi, the historian Firishta, the Venetian traveller Niccolao Manucci, Charles Warren Malet and Captain Seely.

In the 19th century, the Holkars of Indore came to control Ellora, and began charging entrance fees and auctioning rights to worship. After the Holkars, the caves came under the Nizams of Hyderabad and then, finally, were given over to the Archaeological Survey of India.

The most famous monument at Ellora is the great Kailasha temple, whose plinth alone is over 7 m high. It was carved out of a giant monolith freed from its parent hill – an eternal marvel of both engineering and aesthetics.

The Kailasha was impressive enough to deserve imitation shortly after its completion. The Jaina group of excavations at Ellora includes Chhota Kailasha, which is only about a quarter the size of the original, and far less majestic. Perhaps this is because the first Kailasha

was not only the epitome of Indian rock-cut architecture, but was also an augur of its demise. Increasing engineering skills meant that temples would be built up from the ground, virtually anywhere. And so the need to cut temples into hillsides evaporated, signalling the end of this majestic art form.

Brahma, Kailasha temple, Cave 16, Ellora

Other Monuments

Places of interest near Ajanta and Ellora include Aurangabad, Khuldabad, Daulatabad, the Grishneshwar Temple and the Pitalkhora caves.

Besides being the nearest railhead and airport to the World Heritage sites, Aurangabad is also famous for Bibi-ka-Maqbara, the tomb of Rabia-ul-Daurani, Emperor Aurangzeb's wife. Near the city are the Aurangabad caves – 12 Buddhist excavations of some interest.

Khuldabad is worth a visit primarily for Emperor Aurangzeb's grave: a stark affair, open to the skies and left entirely

unmarked until Lord Curzon had a simple railing built around it.

Daulatabad is the site of one of the most impressive forts in the Deccan. It is where Sultan Muhammed-bin-Tughlaq shifted his capital from Delhi in 1327, with such resounding failure.

At Pitalkhora, there are 14 Buddhist caves, located in a valley that is reached after a steep descent and by crossing a beautiful rivulet.

Finally, the Grishneshwar Temple dedicated to the god Shiva, houses one of the 12 *jyotirlingas.* It was built in the 18th century by the Maratha queen, Rani Ahilyabai Holkar.

Bibi-ka-Maqbara, often called the Taj of the Deccan, with its symmetrical Mughal garden

AJANTA CAVES

The first glimpse of the Ajanta caves hidden in a lonely ravine of the Sahyadri Ranges, is awe-inspiring. The caves are cut into a crescent-shaped gorge, nearly 75 m deep, through which flows the stream Waghora. The stream subsequently descends at the head of the ravine beyond Cave 28 in a series of seven waterfalls called Satkund.

The caves at Ajanta, locally called Rangit Leni or painted caves, were excavated as *varshavasa*, retreats for Buddhist monks in the rainy season. The serene setting, far removed from worldly distractions, was fertile ground for the creation of some of the most beautiful representations of the Buddhist faith.

On the walls of the cave-temples are painted a plethora of images ranging from kings and queens to merchants and servants, set against a varied scene of forests, gardens, courts and cities, wide plains and deep jungles, presenting a vivid kaleidoscope of society at the time.

Cave 1 is the first cave that the visitor gets to see as he enters the complex, though it is not the oldest, having been excavated only in the 5th century AD, a good 600 years after the earliest excavations at Cave 10 were initiated. This is because the Ajanta caves have been numbered sequentially rather than chronologically. The caves were excavated in different periods and while the later caves lie on either side of the gorge the older ones are in the middle.

A bejewelled king paying tribute to Bodhisattva Vajrapani, Cave 1

The sculpture of Buddha in the antechamber, Cave 1

Cave 1

Walk into Cave 1 and you realise why Ajanta is so famous. This *vihara* or monastery was excavated during the second phase of activity in 475-500 AD, and contains some exquisite paintings of Bodhisattvas and *Jatakas*. The paintings today are visible only in patches, many of them obliterated by the ravages of time. However, even these are fair indication of the cave in its pristine splendour. The ceiling, too, is profusely decorated with innumerable panels of floral, vegetal and animal motifs, relieved by comic figures and drinking scenes.

A product of Mahayana Buddhism, the cave is covered with painted and carved Buddhas and Bodhisattvas. It has an elaborately carved façade, verandah, hall, side aisles, inner shrine and 14 cells for monks to live in. Structurally, the cave represents a maturing of the *vihara* style: it now becomes a self-contained unit of the monastic establishment with the addition of an inner shrine. Thus monks resided and also practised their rituals within Cave 1.

The cave is decorated with numerous friezes relating stories from Buddha's life. In the verandah is the famous incident of the Ominous Sights – a sick man, an old man and a corpse – encountered by Prince Gautama in the course of his drives through his father's palace grounds.

Bodhisattva Padmapani, on the left of the antechamber of Cave 1, exudes divine radiance

Three richly carved doorways lead into the main hall of the cave. Inside the hall, the ceiling is supported by 20 pillars, each profusely carved with various motifs. Especially noteworthy is one of four deer depicted with one head.

A small antechamber leads to the shrine at the far end of the cave, which contains a colossal image of Buddha seated in the preaching attitude. The figure is remarkable in that it reflects different expressions of Buddha when viewed from different angles.

The highlight of this cave are the two Bodhisattvas painted on the back wall flanking the entrance to the antechamber. The figures attract the viewer with the brilliance of their composition as well as expression. Bodhisattva Padmapani (to the left of the antechamber), holding the sacred lotus in his hand is 'melting in *karuna* and seemingly in motion in the midst of a radiantly moving and rejoicing world'. To the left of Padmapani is probably his consort, a dark beauty who has been depicted with immense grace and charm – note the tips of her nose and lips which have been especially highlighted.

Bodhisattva, the ideal of the Mahayana tradition, is an individual who delays his Enlightenment in order to lead other sentient beings to deliverance.

Bodhisattva Vajrapani (to the right of the antechamber) holds a *vajra* (thunderbolt) in his hand and wears a bejewelled crown which is awe-inspiring in its grandeur. One of the ladies at the bottom of this painting, remarkable for the delicacy of her features, is popularly called the Dark Princess.

On the walls of the antechamber of Cave 1 are depicted two important incidents from Buddha's life. The painting on the left represents the Assault and Temptation of Mara while the one on the right is the Miracle of Sravasti. Both are recurrent images in Buddhist art, and are represented several times in the painting and sculpture at Ajanta.

Assault and Temptation of Mara

For six years Siddhartha roamed the forest seeking the path leading to release from samsara. But that knowledge remained elusive. Finally, on the banks of the Nairanjana river, he sat under a pipal or a Bodhi tree, determined not to leave his vajrasana till he attained supreme knowledge. For the next 49 days Mara, the Evil One, tried his best to distract the Lord – subjecting him to the assault of his army of demons and the temptation of his beautiful and seductive daughters. Eventually, Buddha called upon the Earth as witness to his rightful quest for knowledge, with the bhumisparsa mudra. Piercing the shell of ignorance, he discovered that only by conquering desire can one attain the true path to Nirvana. From then on he was Buddha or the Enlightened One.

Faring far, wandering alone,
bodiless, lying in a cave, is the mind.
Those who subdue it are free from
the bonds of Mara.

***Dhammapada* 37**

Miracle of Sravasti

One of the many miracles performed by Buddha during his lifetime to prove his detractors wrong was in the presence of King Prasenjit of Sravasti. In this instance he multiplied himself a thousand times, poised on lotuses in different postures.

Sibi Jataka

In the Sibi Jataka, Bodhisattva, born as King Sibi, gave shelter to a pigeon being pursued by a hawk. However, the hawk deprived of what he considered his legitimate right, appealed to the king for justice. The righteous king was left with no option but to offer his own flesh equal in weight to the pigeon's, to the hawk. The hawk and pigeon were gods Indra and Agni in disguise, and when they saw that the king was willing to make the supreme sacrifice of his life they revealed themselves to him.

Jatakas are a collection of stories of the previous births of Buddha, reincarnated in human and animal forms. The 547 *Jatakas* or Birth Stories are allegorical tales relating to Buddha's previous births.

Starting from the front wall to the left of the main doorway, is a version of the *Sibi Jataka.* On the left, King Sibi can be seen with a pigeon in his lap while on the right he is standing next to a pair of weighing scales. The expression on the king's face is poignant as he readies to sacrifice his flesh to save the life of the pigeon.

The next panel has been interpreted as representing the Conversion of Nanda.

On the left wall of the hall is painted a palace-scene from *Sankhapala Jataka* which continues on the next pilaster. In the palace-scene the *naga* king is listening to an ascetic, to the right is a serpent-king being dragged by his kidnappers and just below is a man, Alara, ready with his ransom of oxen and coins. At the bottom is Sankhapala leading Alara to his abode in the lotus lake.

The dejected figure of Princess Sundari, from the panel on the Conversion of Nanda, Cave 1

Sankhapala Jataka

Bodhisattva, born as prince of Magadha, wished to be reborn as a naga king whose wealth and splendour dazzled him. Reborn as the naga king Sankhapala, he soon tired of the meaningless life of riches and, by way of atonement, decided to kill himself. He lay on an ant-hill and was tortured by a group of men. Alara, a kind-hearted merchant, finally rescued the serpent-king by paying as ransom his oxen and some gold coins. The grateful Sankhapala took Alara to his aquatic palace and entertained him for a year, and was finally able to influence Alara of the meaninglessness of worldly pleasures.

Left
King Mahajanaka leaving his palace, Cave 1

The *Mahajanaka Jataka* occupies the rest of the left wall. On the extreme left is a princess, Sivali, who along with her attendants is tempting the prince, Mahajanaka. On the right can be seen the prince, who is clearly not enjoying all this mirth. To the left of the sanctum, on the back wall, Mahajanaka is shown taking the ritual bath before donning saffron robes.

Far left
King Mahajanaka being given a ritual bath before renouncing worldly life, Cave 1

Mahajanaka Jataka

Mahajanaka, son of the slayed king of Mithila, grew up to become a rich merchant. During his sojourns he married Sivali, the daughter of the usurper king. However, in course of time, Mahajanaka renounced all worldly pleasures despite the best efforts of his beautiful wife.

The next panel on the left wall of voyage and shipwreck scenes, has been identified as depicting Kalyanakarin's adventures.

Kalyanakarin's Adventures

The generous prince Kalyanakarin was blinded by his wicked younger brother after they had been shipwrecked. In the course of his wanderings a rich princess fell in love with him and they got married. He regained his eyesight by virtue of a satyakriya (solemn profession of truth), and returned with his wife to his own kingdom.

Scenes from the *Champeyya Jataka* can be seen to the right of the antechamber on the back wall of the cave. On the top left is the dejected figure of a *naga* king in his palace. On the right, is depicted the court of the king of Varanasi who has captured the *naga* king. The *naga* queen is seen pleading for the release of her husband.

Champeyya Jataka

Bodhisattva was reborn as the naga king Champeyya. Disgusted with his reptile existence, Champeyya went to the world of men and allowed himself to be caught by a snake charmer. He was finally set free by the king of Varanasi at the request of the naga queen Sumana. Afterwards he took the king of Varanasi to the netherworld and entertained him lavishly for seven days.

***Champeyya Jataka,* Cave 1**

To the right of the court scene, the *naga* king is delivering a discourse to an assembly.

An interesting scene to the right of the main doorway on the front wall shows a royal personage receiving gifts from men in peaked caps and sporting beards. It has been interpreted by some as the Chalukya king, Pulakesin II receiving a delegation from King Khusrau II of Persia. However, it probably represents Emperor Ashoka's reception of foreign embassies.

Cave 2

Cave 2 contains some of the best preserved paintings at Ajanta. Abundantly ornamented, in fact even more so than Cave 1, this monastery was excavated sometime near the beginning of the 6th century.

Flanking the cave are two cells with pillared porches. Above the porch of the right cell is a seated *naga* king with his attendants, while on the left cell is Hariti, the Divine Protectress of Children.

Entry to the hall of Cave 2 is through a richly carved doorway. There are 12

Hariti and her consort, Cave 2

pillars in the hall, some of which seem over-ornamented. Along the side walls of the hall are ten cells. The shrine at the back of the cave has an image of Buddha in the preaching attitude. On either side of the antechamber are subsidiary chapels with remarkably well-preserved paintings. In the right chapel is Hariti with her consort, Panchika, the Lord of Wealth. On the top corner of the sculpture is depicted Hariti's attack on Buddha and her conversion. The chapel on the left has two *yakshas* along with *chamara*-bearers.

Legend has it that Hariti, an ogress or *rakshasi*, was fond of devouring children. Buddha, in an attempt to reform her, hid the ogress's favourite child. Infuriated Hariti attacked Buddha but was eventually converted to his Faith. Buddha assured Hariti that she would get food in any monastery she visited, giving birth to the custom of installing her image in the porch or the dining-room of monasteries in India. She is thereafter always portrayed with a child seated on her lap.

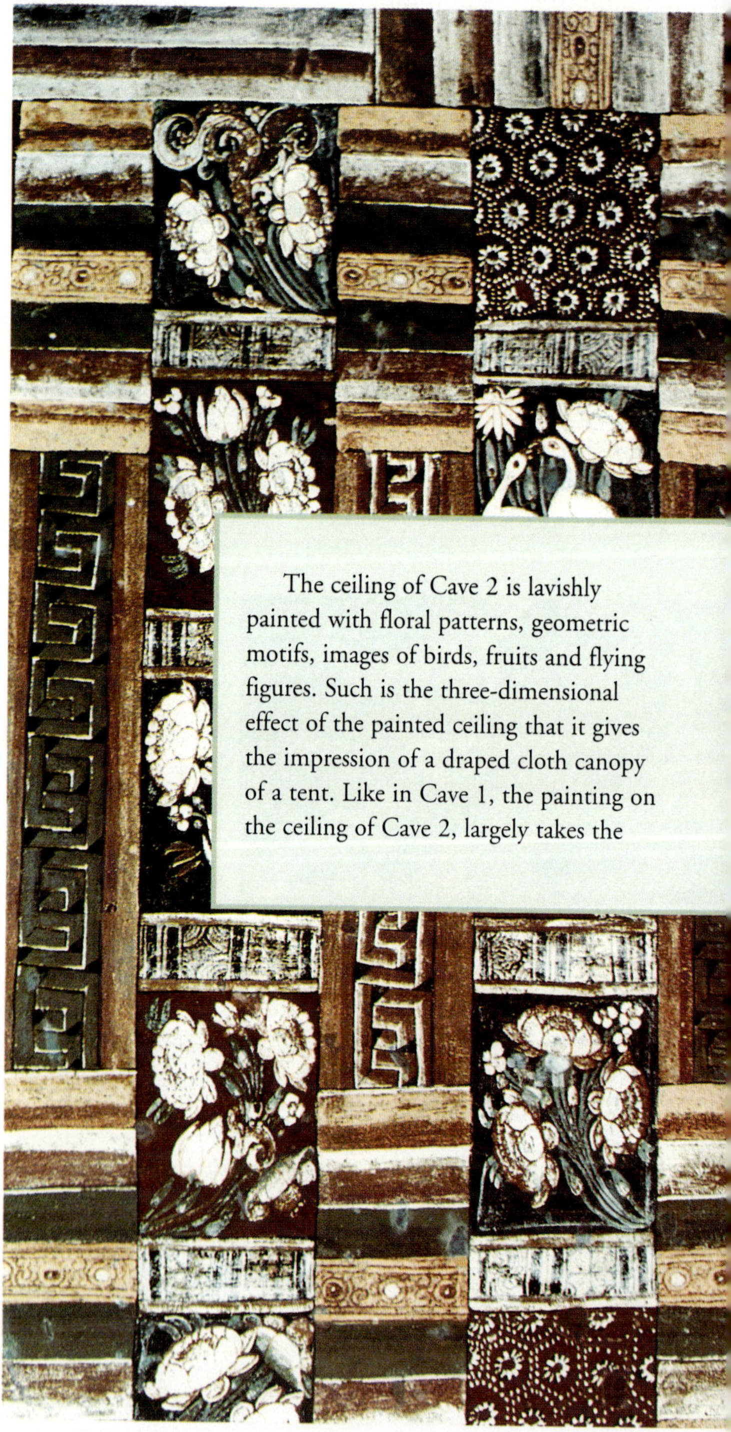

The ceiling of Cave 2 is lavishly painted with floral patterns, geometric motifs, images of birds, fruits and flying figures. Such is the three-dimensional effect of the painted ceiling that it gives the impression of a draped cloth canopy of a tent. Like in Cave 1, the painting on the ceiling of Cave 2, largely takes the

form of squares and rectangles filled with designs. We also find concentric bands filled in with exquisite motifs.

The artists' keen observation skills and masterful execution is visible on the ceiling of the left chapel where there is a procession of 23 geese depicted in various postures.

Birth of Buddha

Buddha's mother, Queen Mahamaya dreamt of a white elephant entering her womb. The court astrologer predicted that the queen would give birth to a male child who would either become a great ascetic or the ruler of the world. After carrying the future Buddha in her womb for ten months, the queen gave birth while standing under a *sala* tree and the infant emerged from his mother's right side.

On the side walls of the shrine and antechamber are painted countless Buddhas that bring to mind the 'Cave of the Thousand Buddhas' at Tun Huang in Central Asia. The episode is referred to as the Miracle of Sravasti. In this miracle, Buddha manifested himself in a thousand different forms to silence disbelievers.

To the left of the shrine doorway is Bodhisattva Avalokitesvara, who protects mankind from the Eight Great Perils of lions, elephants, fires, snakes, thieves, water, fetters and demons. The left wall of the hall is painted with scenes from Buddha's birth.

On the extreme left wall of the hall is painted the *Hamsa Jataka.* To the left of the cell door is a bird-catcher. In the top panel the golden goose, is shown seated on a throne, delivering a sermon to a royal couple.

Hamsa Jataka

A golden goose, Dhritarashtra (Bodhisattva) lived with his flock on Mount Chitrakuta. The queen of Varanasi dreamt of a golden goose preaching to her and requested the king to find the goose. The king made a decoy lake and ordered the bird-catcher to capture the golden goose. Dhritarashtra was brought before the royal court where he gave a discourse to the king and queen and was thereafter set free.

Two comical figures; note the one wearing bright blue socks, Cave 2

Miracle of Sravasti, Cave 2

Scenes from the *Vidhurapandita Jataka* cover a large portion of the right wall of the hall. On the right half of the painting is a princess, Irandati on a swing and a *yaksha*, Punnaka. On the left half is the audience-chamber of a king with a game of dice in progress.

Vidhurapandita Jataka

Punnaka, a yaksha general, was in love with a naga princess, Irandati and wished to marry her. The naga queen, however, set a precondition to the marriage: Punnaka must get her the heart of Vidhurapandita (Bodhisattva), the wise minister of the king of Indraprastha. Punnaka cleverly defeated the king of Indraprastha in a game of dice and won Vidhurapandita as his prize. The minister instead of being frightened by his imminent death actually directed Punnaka on how to remove his heart. The yaksha general struck by Bodhisattva's courage took him to the court of the naga king where Vidhurapandita impressed the naga king and queen with his discourses.

Further to the left is painted the *Mriga Jataka* (also known as *Ruru Jataka*). At the bottom is a spotted deer carrying a person on his back while faint traces of a male and female figure are discernible at the top of the panel.

Mriga Jataka

Bodhisattva was born as a golden deer (mriga) and happened to rescue a drowning man. In the meantime, the queen of Varanasi who had dreamt of a golden deer preaching to her asked the king to find her such an animal. The treacherous man whom the Bodhisattva had rescued told the king of the deer's whereabouts. The king was about to capture the Bodhisattva when the deer began narrating the story of his betrayal to him. Having heard the story, the king wanted to punish the deer's betrayer. However, the Bodhisattva, a symbol of magnanimity, asked the king to forgive the man. The golden deer then gave a discourse to the king and queen of Varanasi.

Caves 3-8

Of caves 3 to 8, only caves 4 and 6 are worth a visit, the rest being mostly incomplete.

The *vihara*, Cave 4, is the largest excavation at Ajanta, and though it was left unfinished, one can see here the various stages of excavation that the cave underwent till final completion. Entry to the cave is through one of Ajanta's most spectacular doorways. It is elaborately carved with figures of Buddha, *ganas, sardulas* with riders, *sala-bhanjikas* and flying couples. On the right of the door is a rectangular panel with a standing figure of Avalokitesvara, while to the left is Buddha depicted in the teaching attitude.

The cells on three sides of the hall are incomplete and in different stages of excavation. In the shrine is a colossal image of Buddha in the teaching attitude, flanked by Bodhisattvas Vajrapani and Padmapani. On the walls of the ante-chamber are six large, carved images of Buddha, of which two are incomplete. These figures along with those in the shrine were originally painted as can be seen from traces which are still visible.

Cave 6 is a two-storeyed monastery. The verandah of its lower storey has entirely disintegrated and most of the decoration on its doorway has crumbled. The cave has a hall, 16 cells, a shrine and an antechamber. In the shrine is a carved image of Buddha detached from the back wall and seated in the teaching attitude. The shrine was originally painted with innumerable figures of Buddha, of which very few remain. On the left wall of the antechamber is painted the Miracle of Sravasti, while on the right is depicted the Assault and Temptation of Mara.

The first floor of the monastery can be reached by climbing a flight of steps to the right of the cave's main entrance. Flanking the verandah of the first floor is a chapel containing an image of Buddha. On this floor is a hall, cells, some of which have pillared porches, a shrine and an antechamber. The shrine contains a carved image of Buddha in the teaching attitude. A profusion of Buddhas carved in different attitudes covers the walls of the hall, antechamber and shrine. Among them a small one on the left wall of the antechamber is so finely covered with lime that it gives the appearance of being carved from marble.

Cave 8 was excavated at a very low level, hence most of it has been swept away, probably by a landslide.

The façade of Cave 9, dominated by a great *chaitya*-window

Cave 9

Cave 9, a *chaityagriha* or prayer hall, was excavated in the 1st century BC during the first phase of excavations.

The cave's façade is dominated by a *chaitya*-window, originally decorated with wooden latticework. The figures of Buddha on the verandah's front and side walls are Later Mahayana additions. The cave is rectangular in shape, and at its centre is a stupa, standing on a high cylindrical base. The stupa is not as decorated as the ones belonging to the second phase of excavations, Cave 19 or Cave 26.

Crowning the stupa is a railing and a *harmika* or finial. As with most caves excavated in the early phase, the use of wooden adjuncts was widespread in Cave 9. The *harmika* was capped by wooden umbrellas as proved by the sockets meant to receive the shafts. Holes in the panels between the pillars and ceiling also suggest that beams and rafters were used to provide superfluous support to the ceiling.

A common practice followed by contemporary artists was to paint over an existing composition without completely erasing it. On the extreme left of the front wall are painted two *bhikshus* below whom is a record stating that it belongs to the 5th century AD. Beneath this is an earlier painting, which depicts two groups of figures separated by rocks. The coiffures, ornaments and costumes of these figures are similar to contemporary reliefs at Sanchi, hence they can be dated to the first phase of excavations at Ajanta.

Another instance where a later artist has painted over an earlier work can be seen in a painting of six Buddhas on the left wall, under which is an earlier painting of devotees heading towards a stupa. The colour scheme, style and workmanship of this painting is in marked contrast to the later painting of the six Buddhas.

Cave 10

In 1819, as Captain John Smith, the British officer credited with rediscovering these caves, delved deeper into the forest in pursuit of a tiger, little did he know that he was going to uncover something so momentous. In front of him was a crescent-shaped gorge and high up on it a tiger, silhouetted against what looked like the carved façade of a cave. This cave was later named Cave 10, and is probably the finest early rock-cut *chaityagriha* to have been excavated in western India.

The cave was also probably the earliest *chaityagriha* at Ajanta. Inside are traces of graffiti dating to its rediscovery. In fact, enthusiatic guides will point to the top of one of the pillars on which the British captain apparently carved his signature soon after discovering the cave.

The cave has the usual nave, apse, aisles and a stupa, and like its neighbour Cave 9, displays predominantly Hinayana influences. The cave's façade, probably made of wood, is missing. The fact that it actually existed is evident from an inscription, which states that the façade was donated by Vasithiputa Katahadi. As was typical of all early caves, in this *chaityagriha* too there is evidence of extensive use of wood in covering the ceiling. In places where wood was not physically used, the architects, not used to working on rocky surfaces, replicated wooden designs, as seen in the rock-cut half-arches of the aisle ceilings.

The stupa in Cave 10 is simple and unornamented. This is unlike the profusely decorated stupas in the *chaityagrihas* excavated during the later phase.

In this cave, as in Cave 9, there are paintings belonging both to the early and later phases of excavations. A painting on the left wall, much damaged by scrawls of errant tourists, depicts the worship of the *Bodhi* tree and the stupa by a king and his retinue. The painting is in a continuous frieze-like band, characteristic of early Ajanta paintings, and has been superimposed by paintings dating to a later period. On the right wall we can see fragments of early paintings covered with later ones. In fact, Buddha figures are often superimposed on earlier decorative motifs.

On the right wall are two *Jatakas*, *Sama Jataka* and *Chhaddanta Jataka*.

The king of Varanasi shooting an arrow. Detail from *Sama Jataka*, Cave 10

Sama Jataka

Bodhisattva, born as Sama, was the only son of his blind parents. One day, while filling water from the river, he was accidentally killed by the king of Varanasi. Such was the sorrow of Sama's parents on losing their son that it moved a goddess to bring him back to life and also restore the eyesight of his parents.

A long, horizontal and damaged frieze represents *Chhaddanta Jataka*. Though the story is not presented in chronological order, the main incidents of the *Jataka* are recognisable: an elephant king, Chhaddanta giving a lotus to another elephant, Queen Mahasubhadda; Subhadda, queen of Varanasi, ordering the hunter, Sonuttara to kill Chhaddanta; Sonuttara showing the tusks to Subhadda; and the queen swooning at the sight of the tusks.

Chhaddanta Jataka

Bodhisattva born as Chhaddanta, a great white, six-tusked elephant, had two wives, Mahasubhadda and Chullasubhadda. Chullasubhadda, jealous of her husband's attentions towards the other wife, prayed that she be reborn as queen of Varanasi to avenge her humiliation. Her wish was fulfilled and she was reborn as Subhadda, queen of Varanasi. Subhadda told her husband, the king, that she wished to possess the six tusks of a white elephant. The king ordered Sonuttara, a hunter, to saw the tusks of such an elephant. The hunter captured Chhaddanta but was unable to cut his tusks. Chhaddanta, despite his wounds, helped Sonuttara saw off his tusks. When the queen was shown the tusks, she remembered the magnificent elephant that her husband had been, and died of grief.

Cave 11-15A

Caves 11-15A would probably be interesting only to those keen to witness the historical progression of the excavations at Ajanta.

Cave 11, a monastery, was excavated in the early 5th century AD. The fact that it was probably part of the initial efforts of the second phase of excavations in Ajanta is attested by its amateurish pillars and irregularly built cells. The verandah ceiling is painted with motifs of flowers, birds, beasts and various geometric designs; however, most other paintings are in quite a damaged condition. The shrine has an image of Buddha in the teaching attitude carved against an unfinished stupa.

The adjacent Cave 12, on the other hand, belongs to the first phase and was probably built around the 2nd century BC. The façade of the cave is in ruins. Within the cave is a square hall with 12 cells ranged on three sides. Each cell has two beds and there are holes in the sills and lintels for pivot-hinges, which were meant for single wooden doors. Though the cave once bore paintings, hardly anything is visible today.

Cave 13, a monastery that is now in a dilapidated state, was excavated around the same time as Cave 12. It has a hall with seven cells on three sides, each of which have two stone beds and one even a raised stone pillow. The cells are so narrow that it is likely that they served only as dormitories. It is probable that this cave was never painted.

Excavated above Cave 13, Cave 14 can be accessed by an ancient staircase. It probably belongs to the second phase.

Kneeling elephant at entrance to Cave 16

Not much survives of Cave 15 as all the pillars of its verandah have fallen; however, on the lintel of the main doorway is a unique two-tiered *sikhara*. The ceilings of the hall, antechamber and shrine show traces of paintings.

Descending the stairs between Caves 14 and 15, to the right, is a small monastery, Cave 15A. This early cave has a hall, which has a single cell on each side. On three sides of the cells are platforms, which probably served as beds.

Cave 16

A door flanked by kneeling elephants leads to a staircase going up to Cave 16. Arguably one of the more beautiful monasteries at Ajanta, the large verandah of the cave offers a stupendous view of the gorge below. An inscription on the walls attributes this magnificent *vihara* to the largesse of a devout Buddhist, Varahadeva, a minister in the court of the Vakataka king, Harishena (*c.* 475-500 AD), during whose reign some of the finest art at Ajanta was created.

Flying couple in the hall of Cave 16

The inscription records that it was built for the use 'of the best of the ascetics' and was therefore adorned with beautiful picture galleries, statues of celestial nymphs and ornamental pillars.

The 20-pillared hall has 14 cells along three sides. The shrine at the rear of the cave has a gigantic carved image of Buddha.

On the left wall of the hall is an incomparable painting, popularly referred to as the 'Dying Princess'. The disconsolate princess is identified as Sundari, the wife of Nanda, whose husband has just been forcefully ordained by Buddha. Nanda's tonsure and his journey through air in the company of Buddha are easily identifiable.

On the front wall of the hall are scenes from the *Hasti Jataka* showing men feeding off an elephant carcass.

Nanda's Conversion

Buddha's half-brother Nanda was enamoured of his beautiful wife, Sundari. When Buddha went to beg for alms at his house he found Nanda assisting his wife with her make-up. Buddha took Nanda to a monastery and forcefully ordained him. The Lord promised the unhappy Nanda heavenly nymphs provided he performed his religious duties zealously. Nanda in the hope of attaining the celestial nymphs applied himself rigorously to self-control. Ridiculed by the other monks for his foolishness, Nanda ultimately realised his folly and renounced all worldly pleasures to become a monk.

Hasti Jataka

Bodhisattva, born as a benevolent elephant, flung himself to death from the top of a precipice so that hungry travellers could feed on his carcass.

The second painting on the left wall of the front aisle has episodes from the *Maha-ummagga Jataka*. This *Jataka* is about a gifted child, Mahosadha, who settled disputes. Starting from the left is delineated the 'Riddle of the Son', where Mahosadha settles a dispute between two persons both claiming to be the mother of a child. In this version of the story

Mahosadha orders that the child be cut into two so that both the claimants can have equal parts. The real mother immediately refuses and Mahosadha is able to decide who the real mother is. Lower down to the right, is the 'Riddle of the Chariot', where two persons claim ownership of a chariot, and Mahosadha declares the rightful owner. The adjoining pilaster shows the 'Riddle of the Cotton-thread', where a woman steals a ball of thread and Mahosadha decides the rightful owner by asking what object has been placed inside the ball.

A detail from *Maha-ummagga Jataka*

Cave 17

A little over half way down the group of caves you reach Cave 17, a monastery that is considered by many to be the most beautiful in Ajanta. Beginning from the verandah and encompassing the walls of the hall and antechamber, this monastery preserves the greatest number of wall paintings and numerous renditions of popular *Jataka* tales. The creative use of colour and freedom of expression in depicting human and animal forms mark this cave as an artistic highpoint. The impression being that the walls were not merely surfaces to be decorated but rather that they offered precious space on which the legends might be depicted for the edification of the devout.

Probably excavated by a feudatory of the Vakataka king, Harishena, it dates to the end of the 5th century AD. The cave has a large verandah in front, which leads into the main hall. On top of the main

***Yaksha* couples above the entrance, Cave 17**

Maitreya, the Future Buddha, above the entrance, Cave 17

doorway is a panel with seven Manushi Buddhas along with Maitreya, the Future Buddha. Also in the verandah, to the left of the doorway, is an interesting painting, which depicts Indra flying in the clouds along with his retinue. The consummate skill of the artist can be clearly seen in the soaring movements of the figures.

The shrine doorway is elaborately carved with a profusion of images. Within the shrine is an image of Buddha flanked by Padmapani and Vajrapani.

Scenes from *Vessantara Jataka*, Cave 17

Starting from the verandah to the left of the door and covering the entire left wall of the hall are scenes from *Vessantara Jataka*. A royal couple, Prince Vessantara and Madri are seen seated within a pillared porch. Next, the sad couple is seen going towards a city-gate, and beyond it Vessantara is seen distributing alms to a large assembly of beggars, mendicants and ascetics.

Vessantara Jataka

Bodhisattva was born in his final incarnation as the generous Prince Vessantara, who donated a magical elephant to the drought-stricken kingdom of Kalinga. This angered his own subjects and Vessantara was banished. The gods who wished to test the limits of his generosity sent an evil brahmin, Jujaka, who asked the prince to donate his children to him. The prince, though immensely pained, nevertheless gave away his children. The children were finally rescued by their grandfather, the king, who paid a huge ransom to Jujaka. Thereafter Vessantara returned to his kingdom at the request of the remorse-stricken subjects.

Flying Apsara, Cave 17

Buddha and Nalagiri

Buddha had a cousin called Devadatta, who conspired many times to kill him. Once while the Lord was walking on the streets of Rajgir, Devadatta let loose a rogue elephant, Nalagiri. The elephant wreaked havoc and destroyed everything that came in its way. However, on reaching Buddha, he miraculously came to a halt and prostrated himself before the Lord.

On the left wall of the verandah is an interesting painting: a wheel, upheld by a pair of green hands, called the 'Wheel of Life'. On the right wall are painted *apsaras* or celestial nymphs, one of these is famously known as the Flying Apsara. It is one of the most refined paintings at Ajanta, the *apsara* depicted flying amidst clouds is an epitome of sophistication with her narrow eyebrows, bejewelled turban, ornate earrings and necklace.

Further right is depicted one of the eight miracles performed by Buddha – the taming of a rogue elephant, Nalagiri.

On the left wall of the hall is *Chhaddanta Jataka,* a version of which is also painted in Cave 10.

Over the window and door of the left wall are painted scenes from *Mahakapi Jataka I.* A king and his followers are shooting arrows at monkeys on a mango tree. On the extreme top are seen the monkeys escaping across the river over the stretched body of another monkey, the Bodhisattva.

Mahakapi Jataka I

Bodhisattva, born as the king of monkeys, lived with his retinue on the banks of the Ganga and ate the delicious fruits of a mango tree. The king of Varanasi, when he heard of the tree, decided to lay siege to it. Bodhisattva, in order to save his followers, made a bridge with a bamboo pole and covered the remaining distance with his body. A rival monkey, Devadatta, took advantage of the opportunity and jumped on the outstretched body of Bodhisattva with such force that it broke his heart. The king touched by this spirit of self-sacrifice brought Bodhisattva down and requested him to give a discourse.

On the left wall of the hall are scenes from *Hamsa Jataka,* a version of which is painted in Cave 1. Episodes from *Vessantara Jataka* depicted in the verandah are also painted on the left wall of the hall. On the lower half of the left wall is painted *Mahakapi Jataka II.*

***Hamsa Jataka,* Cave 17**

At the bottom right corner is a farmer perched on a tree; next, he is on the back of the monkey being lifted out of a pit. Above this is a man pelting stones at the sleeping monkey.

Mahakapi Jataka II

Bodhisattva, born as a monkey, saved a farmer who had fallen into a deep pit. The farmer, instead of being grateful, attempted to kill the monkey while the latter was asleep. Bodhisattva admonished the man for being ungrateful but eventually forgave him.

On the back wall of the cave is painted the *Mahasutasoma Jataka*. On the bottom right corner is a king, Sudasa, sleeping in a forest while a lioness is licking his feet. A little above, the lioness with a child is going towards the palace gate. The king is seen with a child, Prince Saudasa, in his lap. There is also a scene showing the coronation of Prince Saudasa. The cannibalism of Prince Saudasa is indicated in the three adjoining scenes. Next a prince, Bodhisattva, is seen on the shoulders of Saudasa in a lotus-lake.

Mahasutasoma Jataka

In this version of the Mahasutasoma Jataka, Saudasa, the prince of Varanasi born of a lioness, became a cannibal and was driven out by his subjects. Subsequently he started living in the forest and preying on travellers. Bodhisattva, born as Sutasoma a prince of the Kuru kingdom, was captured by Saudasa. Eventually Bodhisattva impressed Saudasa with his courage and also cured the prince of his unnatural love for human flesh.

On the back wall, to the right of the antechamber, are painted four *Jatakas*. In the *Sarabhamiga Jataka*, which occupies the major portion of the wall, Bodhisattva is born as a stag. To the right is the *Machchha Jataka* in which Bodhisattva is born as a fish.

Below the *Sarabhamiga Jataka* is the *Matiposaka Jataka* in which an elephant is seen being led by a royal retinue.

Matiposaka Jataka

Bodhisattva born as a magnificent white elephant was devoted to his blind mother. He once rescued a forester who had lost his way. The man went and told the king of Varanasi about this remarkable elephant. The king subsequently captured Bodhisattva. While in the palace, Bodhisattva, pining for his mother, refused all food. Deeply impressed by the elephant's love for his mother, the king released him.

The *Mahisa Jataka* is painted on the right wall of the antechamber. At the bottom, a monkey is seen putting his hands on the eyes of a buffalo, Bodhisattva; above, the monkey has been dashed to the ground by another fierce looking buffalo.

Mahisa Jataka

Bodhisattva born as a buffalo was tormented by a monkey. However, one day, another buffalo was standing under the same tree and the monkey mistaking him for Bodhisattva started troubling him. The enraged buffalo, unlike the kind Bodhisattva, trampled the monkey to death.

Battle scene from *Simhala Avadana*, Cave 17

On the right wall is painted the *Simhala Avadana*, one of the longest compositions at Ajanta. The story begins at the bottom right end, with a shipwreck scene. Next is the island of *rakshasis* (ogresses) and a man, Simhala, being carried to safety by a horse, Bodhisattva. After which an ogress is seen devouring a king. Between the second and third cell doors is depicted a fierce battle between humans and ogresses. Above this is depicted Simhala's coronation.

The adjoining wall has episodes from *Sibi Jataka*, which is also painted in Cave 1. On the front wall of the hall are painted scenes from *Ruru Jataka*. At the bottom is the king with his retinue of hunters. The next scene depicts the king returning with the deer, carried with great honour on a chariot.

Simhala Avadana

Simhala, a merchant who lived in Simhakalpa, was shipwrecked while on a voyage with 500 other merchants. They were cast on an island inhabited by *rakshasis*. Bodhisattva born as a magical horse helped Simhala escape. However, one of the ogresses followed Simhala to Simhakalpa and killed the king and other palace inmates. Simhala subsequently fought a war against the *rakshasis* and defeated them. He was then crowned king of Simhakalpa.

The rest of the front wall till the door is painted with *Nigrodhamiga Jataka*. The lower part depicts a herd of deer in a park; on the right is an astonished cook, speaking to a king.

Buddha with his son, Rahula, Cave 17

Nigrodhamiga Jataka

Bodhisattva born as a deer was captured with his herd by the king of Varanasi. The king, a voracious eater of deer flesh, killed a deer every day. The deer, to avoid random killing, decided they would choose a victim from amongst themselves by casting lots. Bodhisattva, who had been granted immunity by the king, offered himself as substitute for a pregnant doe. Impressed by this spirit of self-sacrifice, the king granted immunity to all the deer.

The walls of the antechamber are painted with incidents from Buddha's life, such as the Miracle of Sravasti and Buddha's descent at Samkasya in the company of Sakra and Brahma. The rear wall of the antechamber depicts Buddha's wife sending Rahula, their son, to beg his patrimony of Buddha, who, in turn, puts out his begging-bowl.

Cave 19

Cave 19 is one of the most elaborate *chaityagrihas* at Ajanta. It is next to Cave 18, a monastery which is in a completely ruinous state. Extremely well-proportioned, Cave 19 has an exquisitely decorated façade with an elegant pillared portico. Dominating the façade is a *chaitya*-window flanked by *yakshas* beside which are Buddha figures carved in delicate relief. The columns of the front outer walls of the cave are covered with numerous images of standing and seated Buddhas.

Above
A corpulent *yaksha*, façade of Cave19

Right
Beautifully carved image of standing Buddha to the right of the entrance to Cave 19

Façade, Cave 19

Though excavated towards the end of the 5th century AD, the layout of earlier *chaityagrihas* is strictly followed, except for the introduction of the image of Buddha on the stupa. The stupa itself has a unique elongated drum carved with Buddha standing under a decorative arch. Crowning the stupa is a *harmika* and three diminishing *chhatravalis*. From the top of the lower *harmik*a hang garlands.

The seated *naga* king with his consort, Cave 19

Imitation of wooden architecture is seen in the stone ribs of the vaulted ceiling, but the actual use of wood for beams, rafters and the crowning umbrellas seems to have stopped.

Just before entering the cave to the west is a striking image of a *naga* king with seven cobra hoods around his head. His wife, hooded by a single cobra, sits by his side. In front of the *chaityagriha* is a courtyard with side-chapels flanked by two cells.

Caves 20-29

Except for the *chaityagriha,* Cave 26, which is similar in plan and design to Cave 19, the rest of the caves between 20 and 29 are insignificant from the tourist's point of view.

Cave 20, a small unfinished monastery, belongs to the first phase. All the pillars of its verandah have been destroyed over time. The hall has 12 cells and a shrine, which has a seated figure of Buddha. Though most of the paintings of this cave have also perished, on the left wall is a fragment of a panel of Buddha preaching to a congregation. The freshness of the blue colour used in the painting still stands out in the few fragments visible.

Cave 22, a small, incomplete monastery is excavated at a higher level and can be reached by a flight of steps. On the right wall of the shrine are painted the seven Manushi-Buddhas with Maitreya, the Future Buddha. Cave 23 is also a monastery that is quite similar to Cave 21.

If only it had been completed, Cave 24 would probably have been one of the grandest monasteries and the largest after Cave 4. The decorations seen on surviving portions are common in theme but they have been lavishly executed.

A small unfinished monastery, Cave 25, is at a higher level; It does not have a shrine or cells around the hall.

Cave 26, a well-decorated *chaityagriha*, was excavated during the later phase. There is an inscription on the back wall of the verandah that records the gift of the temple of Sugata (Buddha) by a monk, Buddhabhadra. The inscription is dated between 450 and 525 AD.

A profusion of Buddha images adorn the pillars, triforium, façade and interiors of the cave. The cave is similar in its general layout to Cave 19.

The stupa seems to have become only an ornamental object, with the focus of the sculptors having shifted to the decorated plinth, the front of which is carved with the figure of a seated Buddha.

The highlight of this *chaityagriha* is the large figure of the Parinirvana Buddha on the left aisle. Over 7 m long, the figure, with his eyes closed, is lying on a couch.

Below are his disciples mourning the Master's demise, while above him are celestial beings showering flowers, rejoicing at his salvation. Also in the left aisle is a depiction of the Temptation of Mara.

The verandah to the left of the courtyard of Cave 26 leads to Cave 27, which was probably an extension of Cave 26.

Hardly anyone visits the last two caves, 28 and 29, which are not easily accessible.

Part of a panel depicting the Temptation of Mara, Cave 26

ELLORA CAVES

The Ellora caves, known locally as Verul Leni, are located on the Aurangabad-Chalisgaon road, 30 kms from Aurangabad. Home to one of the world's biggest rock-hewn monastic temple complexes, Ellora's greatest marvel is Kailasha – the largest single monolithic excavation in the world.

Ellora's caves are not merely awe-inspiring. When, during the monsoon, every stream is filled with rainwater and the hills are a lush green, the excavations are also unbelievably beautiful.

These hills, rising abruptly from the surrounding plains, are part of the Deccan's Sahyadri Range and are about 65 million years old. The Ellora caves were carved out of a volcanic basaltic formation (in other words, rock made of volcanic deposits) called the Deccan Trap. For a number of reasons, most importantly that this rock is soft when cut but hardens when exposed to the environment, the Deccan Trap proved ideal for excavation. So much so that Maharashtra is dotted with nearly 1,200 caves of varying size and religious affiliation.

Ellora is located on an ancient trade route, which went from Pratishthana (modern Paithan) via Aurangabad, Pitalkhora and Nasik to the ancient ports along the Arabian Sea.

An awe-inspiring *dvarapala* or doorkeeper, Cave 16

The great Kailasha and its grand pillar, the *dhvajastambha*, Cave 16

The caves have been dated to between *c.* 5th-7th centuries AD and 11th-12th centuries AD. They are excavated in the semi-circular scarp of a large plateau, extending from north to south for almost 2 kms. Although nearly 100 caves were excavated, only 34 of these are regularly visited. The right arc on the southern side has the Buddhist group of excavations (Caves 1-12); and the left arc on the north has the Jaina group (Caves 30 to 34); while the Hindu group (Caves 13 to 29) is located at the centre.

All the popular religions of the time are represented in Ellora; and although it is difficult to determine how royal patronage was divided amongst the excavations, archaeologists and historians do have some clues. For example, Kailasha (Cave 16) is attributed to the Rashtrakuta ruler, Krishna I (*c.* 757-83 AD) because of inscriptional evidence on a copper plate grant from Baroda. The inscription says that a great edifice was built on a hill at Elapura (Ellora) by Krishna Raja.

Right
A beautiful seated Buddha at the end of the square-pillared corridor of Cave 12

Below
The entrance to Cave 10

It was so grand, the inscription continues, that even celestial beings were struck by its magnificence. It was as if *sui-generis*, not created by any mortal, and even the architect who designed it was wonderstruck by his own creation.

Patronage of a different kind came to Ellora in the 19th century, when they came to be owned by the Holkars of Indore. The new owners charged an entrance fee and auctioned the right to perform religious ceremonies here. Later, Ellora was handed over to the Nizams of Hyderabad, who carried out extensive repairs. Since Independence, the Archaeological Survey of India has been given charge of the caves.

THE BUDDHIST CAVES

The Buddhists were the first architects in Ellora. Their 12 excavations are dated between *c.* 450 AD and 700 AD. Of these, Caves 1 to 5 are the more ancient.

Cave 2

One of the earliest Ellora caves, this has a pillared *mandapa* flanked by side galleries, and a shrine at the end. The side galleries contain images of Buddha in their sunken niches, many of them unfinished. The shrine itself displays Buddha along with many subsidiary deities. The sculptures, especially the *dvarapalas* (doorkeepers), are massive.

Tourists should plan their visit to Ellora depending on how much time they have. If you have three to four hours, then do visit Caves 12, 16, 21, and Caves 32 and 34. If you have a full day, then plan to scc Cavcs 2, 5, 10 and 12 of the Buddhist group; Caves 14, 15, 16, 21 and 29 of the Hindu group; and Caves 32 to 34 of the Jaina group.

Chaityagriha, Cave 10

Cave 5

The Buddha sculptures of Ellora, though serene, remain bound to Mother Earth

R. S. Gupte

This is a *vihara* (monastery), 36 m deep and 18 m wide. Its most striking features are two long, low stone benches that stretch across its length, flanked by rows of 12 pillars on each side. At its end is a shrine. It also has 20 cells for monks.

Cave 10

Popularly known as Vishvakarma (the celestial architect) or Sutar ka Jhopra (Carpenter's Hut), this cave is visited by local carpenters, who come to worship Buddha as Vishvakarma, their patron deity. Its entrance is a gate, cut through the rock, which leads into an open courtyard, flanked by two storeys of cells. Beyond the courtyard is the shrine, a *chaityagriha*, 25 m long, 13 m wide and 10 m high.

There is a grand *chaitya*-arch before the *chaityagriha*, which seems to have evolved from the horseshoe arches of earlier *chaityas* into a trefoil decoration.

The complex also has a large stupa, nearly 8 m high. Its roof, a huge arch, shows imitations of wooden ribs beautifully rendered in stone. A massive Buddha in the *dharmachakra pravartana mudra* sits in front of the stupa.

Cave 12 (Teen Tal)

This three-storeyed *vihara* is the largest in Ellora, and perhaps even in all of the region.

The first floor has a shrine towards its end; and many sculptural representations of Buddha and subsidiary deities have been used to adorn its walls.

Buddha's *Asanas* and *Mudras*

Of the 179 sculptures of Buddha in Ellora, 112 show him in the *padmasana* (meditating on a lotus seat); 52 show him in the *pralambapada asana* (seated on a stool); and 13 show him standing on a lotus.

The *mudras*, or hand gestures of Buddha are equally varied. The ones most commonly seen in Ellora include the *dharmachakra pravartana mudra* (Buddha preaching the First Sermon and thus setting the Wheel of the Law in motion); the *bhumisparsa mudra* (Buddha calling on the Earth as witness against the evil of Mara); and the *dhyana mudra* (the attitude of deep meditation).

Manushi Buddhas carved on the wall of Teen Tal, Cave 12

Water cisterns
Almost all these caves have provisions for storing water. Ingenious methods were used to harvest rainwater during the monsoon. Often channels were cut into the rock to divert the rainwater into cisterns for use during the dry months.

A staircase leads to the second floor where there is a huge hall, measuring 36 m by 10 m. Thirteen cells have been carved into the end of the hall and its back wall. A shrine placed in the east has a giant Buddha in the *bhumisparsa mudra*, the pose in which he called on Earth to be his witness against Mara's evil forces. This sculpture is flanked by rows of five Bodhisattvas.

The top floor is almost as large as the one below, with a shrine and a huge antechamber to its east. Its back wall has 14 representations of Buddha: to the north, seven images in the *bhumisparsa mudra* and to the south, seven divine Buddhas. The shrine itself has a colossal image of Buddha flanked by Bodhisattvas Padmapani and Vajrapani.

THE HINDU CAVES

The 17 Hindu excavations on the west face of Ellora stretch across almost one kilometre and are dated to between *c.* 650 AD and 900 AD.

Because the Hindu excavations followed immediately after the Buddhist ones, the early Hindu architecture resembles its Buddhist counterpart. With time, however, these carved temples evolved from simple cells with a *mandapa* into more complex cells with *pradakshina pathas* (paths encircling the main shrine, designed for ritual circumambulation) and elaborate *mandapas*.

Mahayogi Shiva, Cave 16

Cave 14 (Ravana ki Khai)

It is unclear how this cave got its unusual name, Ravana ki Khai (Ravana's Abode). However, the excavation is a gigantic pillared courtyard before a shrine that holds a *linga*. The aisles of the courtyard lead to a circumambulatory passage around the shrine. The walls of these aisles are decorated with sculptural representations from the Shaiva and Vaishnava traditions, including an imposing sculpture of Shiva killing the elephant-demon.

Cave 15 (Dasavatara)

Named Dasavatara after the ten incarnations of Vishnu, this is where, for perhaps the first time in Ellora, architects attempted carving a monolithic structure from solid rock. This experiment resulted in a two-storeyed *mandapa* before the cave. The excavation also has two floors, and both contain huge bas-reliefs of various gods and goddesses.

Animal frieze on the plinth, Cave 16

Shiva the destroyer, Cave 16

Cave 16 (Kailasha)

Kailasha is the culmination of the experiment in rock-cut architecture that began with Cave 15. Perhaps India's (and the world's) largest cave excavation, this marked a departure from all the earlier conventions of architecture.

To create this awe-inspiring structure, three deep trenches were sunk into the parent rock, which freed a gigantic monolith, 84 m long, 47 m wide and 33 m high. The architects then carved a temple into this massive chunk of rock.

Kailasha's magnificence is in direct proportion to the grandeur of the patronage that conceived it. It was excavated under Krishna I, a Rashtrakuta monarch who had just subdued the western Chalukyas and was at the height of his power.

> The silent rock can speak more eloquently than the sacred scriptures
>
> **R. S. Gupte**

Kailasha can be divided into four parts: entrance gateway, body, an intermediate Nandi shrine, and the cloisters surrounding its courtyard.

The entrance, carved into the front wall, is a two-storeyed *gopura* made in the Dravidian style. The wall is adorned with sculptures of Shiva, Vishnu and the *Ashtadigpalas* (guardian gods of the eight directions). Its back, too, is decorated with beautiful sculptures of Mahishasuramardini, Vishnu and Kama, the god of Love. To its south is a huge subterranean cistern.

Just into the cave, there stands a grand sculpture of Gajalakshmi; and, a little further, on either side, the temple's courtyard. Most impressive in the courtyard are two great, monolithic elephants and the square pillars on either side. Fourteen meters high, these pillars are crowned with huge *trishulas* (tridents).

To its north, the courtyard has a shrine, sunk into the rock and embellished with images of the three river goddesses – Ganga, Yamuna and Sarasvati.

The main temple's massive plinth is almost 8 m high and its central frieze is carved with elephants, lions and mythical creatures. Episodes from the *Mahabharata*, the *Ramayana* and Krishna's life are sculpted on its walls. The principal shrine rises almost 23 m over the plinth, and has five subsidiary shrines. Inside, there is a pillared *mandapa;* an antechamber and a *garbhagriha* (sanctum sanctorum).

Fragments of paintings still exist on the ceilings, and can be distinguished as two layers – the first from Rashtrakuta times and the second dating to the Holkars, under whom the entire structure was washed in lime and covered with ochre-coloured paintings.

Elaborate sculptural decorations on Cave 16

Panoramic view of the entrance to Kailasha temple, Cave 16

The *mandapa* is breathtaking. Its pillars are exquisitely carved and an outstanding depiction of Nataraja adorns its ceiling. The ceiling is also decorated with murals, most of which have lost their lustre because of soot and carbon deposits.

One can only marvel at the passion of these artists, who must have worked by the light of oil lamps, lying on scaffolding and having to protect themselves from falling dust and stone particles that could easily blind them.

The antechamber between the *mandapa* and the shrine has a huge monolithic *linga* over a *yonipitha*, and its ceiling is embellished with an enormous lotus.

Before the main temple is a Nandi *mandapa*. The style and execution of this monolith indicates that it was sculpted elsewhere and transported here.
The Nandi *mandapa* contains beautiful paintings of stories from the *Ramayana*.

From the Nandi *mandapa*, you can go to the second floor of the *gopura* over the main entrance and catch a glimpse of the cave complex from a window. Two exits from the *gopura* lead to an elevated platform that offers a fuller view of the temple.

A bridge connects the main shrine with the Nandi *mandapa*, and below it are two enormous sculptures of Shiva. The passage leads back to the courtyard which has, to the east, a corridor filled with sculptures.

Located just below the rock's huge overhang, this corridor has marvellous representations of deities, including those of Shiva, Parvati, Vishnu, and Brahma.

No visit is complete without a tour of the Lankeshwara shrine dedicated to Shiva. Located to the north of the main shrine and exquisitely carved, this is probably a later addition.

> The Kailasha is an illustration of one of those rare occasions when men's minds, hearts and hands work in unison towards the consummation of a supreme ideal
>
> **Percy Brown**

Cave 21 (Rameshvara)

Located midway between Caves 16 and 29, this is supposed to be the earliest of the Hindu excavations. It is famous for its sculptures and is uniquely beautiful.

Rameshvara is dedicated to Shiva, who is worshipped in the form of a *linga*. A Nandi is placed just before the cave, over a raised platform. Inside, there is a rectangular *mandapa* and a sanctum.

The walls of the *mandapa* and two cells (one each to its north and south) have massive sculptures.

The shrine's entrance is very elaborate, divided into segments and profusely carved. It is guarded by two *dvarapalas*. The sanctum has a *linga*; and a circumambulatory passage has been scooped out of the rock around it.

Cave 29 (Dumar Lena)

The Dumar Lena cave is near Sita ki Nahani, a pleasant pool created by a waterfall in the Elaganga River during the monsoon. The cave has an isolated shrine within a group of halls arranged in a cruciform, similar to the style of architecture on Elephanta Island, near Mumbai.

The shrine has four entrances, each guarded by grand *dvarapalas*, leading to a *linga*. To its north and south, the cave has two sculpted depressions. These are an enigma, because nobody has yet identified what they were meant for. Various theories have been proposed, prominent among them is that these are Vedic altars, used

THE JAINA CAVES

The Jainas were the last to arrive at Ellora and only five of the excavations here (Caves 30-34) are dedicated to the faith. They are dated between the 9th and 11th-12th centuries AD and Cave 32 (Indra Sabha) and Cave 33 (Jagannath Sabha) are considered most important. Interestingly, Cave 30 is an unfinished imitation of Kailasha and called Chhota Kailasha (literally, Little Kailasha).

The God of Wealth, Matanga, on the first floor of Cave 32

Cave 32 (Indra Sabha)

Cave 32, also called Indra Sabha, has a series of shrines dedicated to Mahavira and other Jaina divinities, aesthetically arranged on two floors. Its main entrance is through a Dravidian *gopura*, which leads to a small courtyard. At its centre is a monolithic shrine on a high pedestal, flanked by a huge pillar called *manastambha* to its right, and a colossal elephant to its left. The elephant is reminiscent of those in Kailasha, but is more elegant and

The Goddess of Wealth and Prosperit Siddhayika, Cave 32

The central shrine is reached by a flight of steps. At its centre is the Sarvatobhadra – in accordance with the Jaina tenet of worshipping the four important *tirthankaras*. The images of these *tirthankaras* are placed at the four cardinal directions.

An exit to the west of the shrine leads to two smaller shrines dedicated to Mahavira. A small exit in the southwest corner goes to a huge shrine of Mahavira. Its pillars and walls are decorated with sublime sculptures. The pillars are elaborate and have evolved from earlier traditions.

AURANGABAD AND AROUND

Although Ajanta and Ellora are the reason most tourists visit Aurangabad, the town and its environs too are not without interest. Originally called Khirki, Aurangabad was renamed by the emperor Aurangzeb, under whom it became an important centre for Mughal rule in the Deccan.

Most notable in Aurangabad is the tomb of Aurangzeb's wife, Bibi-ka-Maqbara and, a few kilometres out of town are the Aurangabad caves, which though less impressive than those at Ajanta and Ellora are nevertheless worth a visit.

A little further is the famous Daulatabad Fort, 15 kms from Aurangabad, and about half-way to Ellora. A visit to the Fort can easily be combined with a trip to Ellora, which is also only a little distance from the Grishneshwar Temple, the site of one of the 12 *jyotirlingas*, and an important place of pilgrimage for Hindus.

The town of Khuldabad, just 3 kms from Ellora, also makes for an interesting excursion, because it is where Emperor Aurangzeb is buried, and also for its many *dargahs* of renowned Sufi saints.

The Pitalkhora caves, however, require a somewhat longer detour, being 40 kms west of Ellora. These isolated and ancient Buddhist excavations are beautifully located across a lovely stream and a visit, if possible, will be pleasant.

Bibi-Ka-Maqbara

Bibi-ka-Maqbara, Aurangabad. Modelled on the Taj Mahal it was built by Azam Shah, son of Aurangzeb

Although the stern emperor Aurangzeb had ordered a tomb as simple as his own for his wife, Rabia-ul-Daurani, their son Azam Shah built her a grander mausoleum – the Bibi-ka-Maqbara.

Built between 1651 and 1661, the tomb was intended to rival the Taj Mahal, but declining architectural standards gave it a somewhat 'squashed' appearance and it does not bear comparison to Agra's more famous tomb.

Judged on its own merits, however, the Maqbara has many pleasing features, not least of all its location, set against a U-shaped gap in the hill range behind it. Rabia-ul-Daurani's grave itself is enclosed with a beautifully designed octagonal marble screen.

Aurangabad Caves

The 12 Buddhist caves of Aurangabad are dated between *c.* 2nd - 3rd centuries AD and the 7th century AD. The most remarkable of these is Cave 7, which is renowned for the beautiful representations of Avalokitesvara and Bodhisattva on either side of the entrance to the shrine. On the inside wall is a striking sculptural panel of a dancing girl surrounded by five female musicians playing different instruments.

Daulatabad Fort

The famous medieval fortress of Daulatabad sits atop an enormous volcanic outcrop that rises steeply from the plains around it to a height of over 200 m.

The powerful Yadava ruler, Bhillama V founded the fortress of Deogiri or the 'Hill of the Gods' in 1187 and made it his capital.

So impressed was Sultan Muhammad-bin-Tughlaq by the impregnable fort that he not only shifted his court and capital from Delhi to Daulatabad but also ordered Delhi's entire population to march the 1,100 kms to their new capital. This harrowing trek caused immense misery and suffering, and 17 years later, facing drought and famine, the Sultan changed his mind and ordered everyone to march back to Delhi.

The fort's design exploited the topography of its location. The lower slopes of its hill were scraped to make a vertical cliff that made the fort unassailable for invading armies. The fort's intricate defence system included three encircling walls with bastions; spikes on gates to prevent the entry of elephants; a deep moat infested with crocodiles; cannons with massive firepower placed at strategic locations; secret labyrinthine tunnels to reach the summit; and smoke chambers emitting toxic gases.

The Jami Masjid is the oldest Islamic monument in Daulatabad Fort. Seen high above it is the 12-pillared *baradari* or summer house built for Emperor Shah Jahan in 1636

The spectacular Chand Minar in Daulatabad Fort is a fine minaret in the Turkish style

Daulatabad is also noteworthy for being the first example of Islamic architecture in southern India; and the fort contains many remarkable buildings, of which the most notable are the Chand Minar, the Jami Masjid and the Chini Mahal.

Built by Sultan Ahmed Shah II, in 1447, the Chand Minar is a remarkable specimen of Islamic architecture. The red sandstone victory tower, 70 m high and 21 m in circumference originally had glazed Persian tiles arranged in intricate geometric patterns on its façade. Though most of the ornamentation has disappeared, the structure remains impressive.

The Jami Masjid, opposite the Chand Minar, was erected by the Delhi sultans in 1318 and comprises 106 pillars taken from the Hindu and Jaina temples previously located here. It has been reconverted and is now known as the Bharat Mata temple.

The Chini Mahal, 'Chinese Palace', decorated with painted tiles, is where Abul Hasan, the last Qutub Shahi ruler of Golconda, was imprisoned by Aurangzeb in 1687. Near it, half way up the fort, sits a massive 17th century cannon, the Kila Shikan or 'Fort Breaker'. It is popularly known as Ram Cannon, because its fuse end is shaped like a ram's head.

Almost near the top is the *baradari* that offers magnificent views of the surrounding area. A further flight of steps leads up to the level summit of the citadel where lies a heavy cannon of the 18th century in its original mountings.

Grishneshwar Temple

Built by Queen Ahilyabai Holkar, who ruled from Indore from 1765-95, the Grishneshwar Temple has one of the twelve *jyotirlingas* in the country.

Built with red basalt, the temple's most striking feature is a five-tiered *shikhara* rising in diminishing height, and crowned with a couchant bull with a monkey behind it on each corner. The *shikhara* is beautifully decorated with geometric motifs and images of Hindu deities, including those of Shiva and Parvati.

During the festival of *Mahashivaratri*, a massive fair is held that draws large crowds.

Khuldabad

Emperor Aurangzeb's grave, the main attraction of the town of Khuldabad, betrays no flamboyance or refinement. It is as stark as his father's mausoleum, the Taj Mahal, is resplendent.

Not only did the ascetic emperor choose to be buried in an unmarked grave, he also insisted on paying for it himself, with the four-and-a-half rupees he earned knitting prayer caps.

The simplicity of the grave so shocked Lord Curzon, Viceroy of India when he visited the site over 200 years later that he instructed the then Nizam of Hyderabad to construct a marble screen around it.

To this day, however, it remains open to the sky. A *tulsi* plant grows on it – an unforced embellishment, in some ways more moving than all the artistry of the world.

After Muhammad-bin-Tughlaq's disastrous relocation of his capital, the 1400 Sufis who are said to have accompanied him south, stayed on in Khuldabad making it one of the Deccan's most important Sufi centres.

Today, the *dargahs* of the many Sufi saints in Khuldabad, among them Sheikh Burhanuddin Gharib and his disciple Sheikh Zaynuddin Shirazi, attract thousands of pilgrims. A hair, said to be of the Prophet Muhammad, is preserved in Burhanuddin's shrine; while Zaynuddin's tomb contains a robe, passed down through generations of Chishti saints and believed to have belonged to the Prophet.

Dvarapalas carved on the entrance to Cave 4, Pitalkhora

Pitalkhora Caves

Pitalkhora's 14 caves were excavated in the Hinayana phase, but painted in the Mahayana phase

The Pitalkhora caves, also called the 'Brazen Glen', are approached by a diversion of 4 kms from Kalimath on the Aurangabad-Chalisgaon road. Visitors must climb down steep steps to reach the caves. A lovely stream runs across the path, and an iron bridge has been built across it.

Pitalkhora is among the region's earliest centres of rock-cut architecture; and was mentioned as 'Petrigala' by Ptolemy. These caves were carved in softer, somewhat fragile rock; so they highlight imaginative examples of 'ancient conservation'. For example, to prevent water seepage, ancient architects bored long tunnels into the ceilings of Cave 4, through which water would flow underneath the cave floor into concealed drains.

PRACTICAL INFORMATION

Excavated in east Maharashtra are two separate groups of Buddhist, Jaina and Hindu caves. Dated from between approximately 200 BC to 1100 AD, they are magnificent examples of religious art: their walls painted with beautiful images and their rock carved into imposing sculptures. Popularly called the Ajanta and Ellora caves, they are located 106 and 30 kms respectively from Aurangabad, the nearest airport and railhead.

WHEN TO COME TO INDIA

Ajanta caves lie in Maharashtra, which is in west-central India. Unlike northern parts of India, which have extremes of climate both in winter and summer, most parts of Maharashtra have a temperate climate. The summer months from March to May see a maximum of 35°C, while during the winter months from October to February temperatures can drop to a minimum of 10-12°C. Monsoons lash the state from July to September.

The best time to visit the caves at Ajanta would undoubtedly be in the rainy season when the region turns a verdant shade of green. The Sahyadri Ranges, where the Ajanta caves are situated, receive the maximum rainfall in the region. In case you cannot visit Ajanta during these months the other good time would be from October to March, when the weather is very pleasant.

What to wear

There is no fixed dress code in India. The sari is the main attire of Indian women, but the easy-to-wear salwar kameez with dupatta is also commonly worn. The kurta and pyjama, with sandals or leather chappals is a typical attire worn by Indian men. However, in large cities western outfits such as trousers, shirts and skirts are common.

For the foreign traveller the thumb rule would be to wear sensible, comfortable clothes that do not attract unnecessary attention. While travelling to western parts of India, loose cotton clothing is apt through the year though light woollens will be required for the winter months.

Before coming to India

There are a few things you need to take care of before travelling to India.

Visa

The tourist visa is normally given for six months. The 15-day single/double-entry visa is issued only to bonafide transit passengers. Tourist groups of not less than four people travelling under the auspices of a recognised travel agency may be considered for a collective tourist visa.

A visa is given for a period for which the passport is valid. So, if the validity of the passport runs out before the visa expires, the visa is not issued. The visa is valid for 180 days from the date of its issue and not from the date of entry into India, unless specified otherwise.

Visa Extension

The 180-day tourist visa is supposedly non-extendable but can be extended for another 15 days in exigencies. A valid onward ticket must, however, be produced as proof of the intention to depart from India's shores. The 15-day extension on the 6-month visa is issued by the Foreigners' Regional Registration Office (FRRO) and can be obtained from any of the offices at New Delhi and Mumbai. The FRRO office is open on weekdays from 9.30 am to 1.30 pm and 2 pm to 4 pm. A 15-day extension is given only if confirmed air tickets are not available. No fees are charged.

STD CODES	
Bangalore	080
Chennai	044
Delhi	011
Kolkata	033
Mumbai	022

FRRO Offices

- **New Delhi**
  East Block 8, Level-II
  Sector-1, R K Puram
  Ph 011-26711443
- **Mumbai**
  Dy. Commissioner of Police Special Branch to CID,
  Annexe-II,
  3rd Floor,
  BT Road, Behind
  St. Xaviers College
  Ph 022-22621169

Registration for foreigners in other towns and cities can be done in the police commissioner's office.

Travel Insurance

Take a travel insurance policy, covering theft and loss, before coming to India. Also buy a medical insurance.

Driving License

A valid International Driving License is necessary if you wish to drive a car or a motorcycle in India, and it is advisable to get one before coming. If you do not have an International Driving License and still wish to drive in India, you can get a Temporary Driving License, provided you are carrying a valid driving license of your country.

HEALTH

Your health during your travel in India depends on three things: Precautions taken before arrival, day-to-day care and efficiency in tackling emergencies.

No particular vaccination is required for coming to India. However, visitors from designated countries in Africa, South America and from Papua New Guinea, even if they are on transit, are required to bring valid Yellow Fever vaccination certificates.

In the absence of this certificate they will be quarantined for six days.

Precautionary medication is the best bet against common ailments like diarrhoea, dysentry and malaria. Malaria is a problem in India during the rainy season. So, if you are coming at that time of the year, do consult your doctor for precautionary anti-malarial medication. While in India, use mosquito repellent.

If you are not already vaccinated against Hepatitis B, get it done before travelling.

For travel health, take care of what you eat and drink. Water is suspect; therefore, it is best to carry your own mineral water. Bottled mineral water, aerated drinks, hot tea and coffee are easily available and are a good substitute for water. Guard against sun-stroke and dehydration, especially if you are travelling during the summer months. It would be useful to keep a packet of oral rehydration salts along with you, and at the first sign of any kind of fatigue or dehydration, to mix its contents in water and sip it frequently.

Time Zone

Indian Standard Time (IST) is 5 ½ hours ahead of Greenwich Mean Time and 10 ½ hours ahead of US Eastern Standard Time. IST is 4 ½ hours behind Australian Eastern Standard Time, 3 ½ hours behind Japanese Standard Time and 1 ½ hours behind Thai Standard Time. Despite its vast geographical territory, India has just one time zone and no daylight saving time in winter.

Hospitals

All Indian metros have government as well as privately-run hospitals and nursing homes. The government hospitals have modern medical facilities, but due to large patient turnout, medical assistance is slow, a fact compensated for by the nominal charges.

THINGS YOU CAN BRING INTO INDIA

Visitors can bring in articles for personal use, including cameras with five rolls of film, a reasonable quantity of jewellery, a pair of binoculars, a portable musical instrument, a portable radio, a tape recorder, a portable typewriter, a laptop computer and professional equipment. On arrival, you will have to give an undertaking on a Tourist Baggage Re-Export (TBRE) form, available with Customs officials at the airport, that you will take these items back when you leave. This form along with the articles that are entered in it, have to be shown to the Customs officials at the time of departure.

Designated 'high-value articles' are also allowed in, but on a written undertaking that they will be taken back at the time of departure. Please obtain a Landing Certificate if you are expecting unaccompanied baggage and for mishandled baggage. You can bring in 200 cigarettes (or 50 cigars or 250 gms of tobacco) and liquor and wines up to 32 oz (1 litre).

You are allowed to bring in any amount of foreign currency in cash or travellers' cheques. However, if you are carrying more than US$5000 (or equivalent), you have to declare it on arrival. Fill up the Currency Declaration Form (CDF) which is to be attested by the Customs Officer.

THINGS YOU CAN TAKE BACK

Export Regulations: A visitor can take back the following goods:

- Souvenirs (including Indian silk, wool, handicrafts, etc.) without any limit.
- Gold jewellery and silverware up to a value of Rs 1,00,000 and in excess of that only after obtaining a permit from the Reserve Bank of India.
- Other jewellery and precious stones (but if of high value, these should be appraised by the Customs Appraiser at the airport before departure).

As a general rule, get a RBI permit for goods of high value. There are restrictions on the export of antiques and art objects which are more than 100 years old. In case of doubt, consult the Director, Antiquities, Archaeological Survey of India, Janpath, New Delhi (Ph 011-23017443). It is advisable to get a certificate of proof. Export of most wildlife products is either prohibited or strictly regulated by the Wildlife Protection Act 1972. Do not buy articles made of ivory, reptile, tiger or deer skin, tortoise-shell or shahtoosh shawls, which are made by killing the Tibetan antelope.

Indian currency cannot be brought in or taken out of the country.

Tax Clearance Certificate

A foreign passport holder staying for more than 120 days (four months), from the date of issue of the visa, regardless of the date of entry into India, would be required to furnish a tax clearance certificate to leave the country. The certificate can be obtained from the Income Tax office in any of the major metropolitan cities.

Earlier, a Foreign Travel Tax was levied on all travellers leaving the country. This tax has been recently abolished.

MONEY

Indian Currency

Indian currency is called the Rupee. It is available in denominations of 1000, 500, 100, 50, 20, 10, 5, 2, 1. One rupee equals 100 paise. Coins in common use are those of Rs 5, Rs 2, Re 1 and 50 paise. The 25, 20 and 10 paise coins have become redundant in big cities, but they still have value in smaller towns and in rural India.

Credit Cards

Credit cards are becoming increasingly popular in urban areas. All major international credit cards including Visa, Amex, Mastercard and Diners Club are used.

Banks

Banks are open from 10 am to 2 pm, Monday to Friday, and 10 am to 12 pm on Saturdays. Most of them, however, remain closed on Sundays and national holidays. Major cities have ATM machines set up by banks. However, when travelling to smaller towns it is advisable to carry necessary cash because you may not find ATMs.

COMMUNICATIONS

Telephone

Public telephone booths are located even in remote areas. ISD (international calls), STD (domestic long distance calls), and local calls can be made from these booths .

DO NOT ACCEPT SOILED CURRENCY NOTES

Pre-paid Telephone Cards

The state-run MTNL now offers facilities for buying pre-paid STD/ISD cards, which the consumer can use to make calls from any phone.

Mobile Phones

All travellers to India, except those from USA, Korea or Japan can use their mobile sets in India. Those coming from the aforementioned countries need to have GPRS-GSM enabled sets. You can use your cell-phone in most places by buying a pre-paid SIM card from the local network service provider.

E-mail

Internet hubs are a common sight in Indian cities. Internet browsing is relatively cheap and costs around Rs 20-30 per hour.

Post Offices

The main post offices in large towns provide a wide range of facilities, like telegraph, fax and a courier service, which operates under the brand name EMS-Speed Post.

New Delhi

The Delhi airport is called the Indira Gandhi International Airport. It has two terminals: Terminal 1 (Domestic) and Terminal 2 (International). The two terminals are 7 kms apart. Terminal 2 is located about 19 kms from the city centre (Connaught Place).

Airport Enquiry

Domestic Terminal
Ph 011-25675121/
25675126

International Terminal
Ph 011-25652011/
25652021

Airlines Offices

Air India
Jeevan Bharati Building,
124 Connaught Circus
Ph 011-23731225
Airport Ph 011-25696621

Indian Airlines
F Block,
Malhotra Building,
Opp. Palika Bazar No. 6,
Janpath Hotel
Ph 1407/011-23310517
Airport Ph 1400/1402
011-25675121

Jet Airways
13 Community Centre,
Opp. Col. Raj's School,
Yusuf Sarai
Ph 011-51641414/
51642424
Airport Ph 011-25675404

Sahara India Airlines
3rd Floor
Dr. Gopal Das Bhawan,
28 Barakhamba Road,
Connaught Place
Ph 011-23326851
Airport Ph 011-25675234

Mumbai

Earlier known as Bombay, Mumbai is the commercial hub of India and, therefore, extremely well connected by air and rail to most parts of the country. Mumbai airport has two terminals; the **Chhatrapati Shivaji Maharaj International Airport,** 29 kms from the city centre at Nariman Point, and the domestic terminal, some 6 kms from the international terminal.

Airport Enquiry

Domestic Terminal
Ph 022-25675121/ 25675126
International Terminal
Ph 022-25652011/ 25652021

Airlines Offices

Air India
Air India Building
218 Back Bay Reclamation
Nariman Point
Ph 022-22024142
Airport Ph 022-28366767

Indian Airlines
Air India Building
218 Back Bay Reclamation
Nariman Point
Ph 022-22023031/3288
Airport Ph 022-26156633/ 26156943

Jet Airways
B-1 Amarchand Mansion
Madame Cama Road, Colaba
Ph 022-22855788
Airport Ph 022-26156666

Sahara
7 GF Tulsiani Chambers
Nariman Point
Ph 022-22835671/5672
Airport Ph 022-26156363/ 26156102

ARRIVING IN INDIA

There are several international airports in India, however, the majority of international air traffic is handled by the New Delhi and Mumbai airports.

Customs

There are two channels for customs clearance at international terminals in Indian airports: Green Channel and Red Channel.

Green Channel: This is for unhindered exit from the airport. You can walk through the Green Channel if you are not carrying goods which attract customs duty.

Red Channel: For those who have anything to declare, including money worth more than US$ 5000.

There are three important domestic airlines operating in India – Indian Airlines, Jet Airways and Sahara Airlines. These handle most domestic flights.

Hand Baggage: In all domestic flights, passengers are allowed one piece of hand baggage. All baggage is subject to security check whether carried by hand or booked in the hold.

Baggage Allowance: Domestic airlines allow 20 kgs check-in baggage for Economy Class and 30 kgs for Business Class. Excess baggage is charged as per the schedule available at the airlines' counter.

Onward or return reservations must be reconfirmed whenever there is a break of journey of over 72 hours.

The reporting time for all domestic flights is 60 minutes prior to departure. Gates close 30 minutes before the scheduled time of departure.

TRAVEL WITHIN INDIA

By Train

The Indian Railways run a gigantic, modern and organised network that connects the metros to most major and minor destinations within India. Trains in India are very crowded and it is necessary to reserve a seat or a berth if you want to travel in any degree of comfort. It is best to buy tickets from the Railway Reservation Offices.

New Delhi

Delhi has three railway stations, the New Delhi Railway Station (RS), Hazrat Nizamuddin RS, and Old Delhi RS.

Railway Enquiry
Ph 131, 1330, 1335, 125050

Mumbai

Mumbai has three main railway stations, namely Mumbai Central, Mumbai CST (formerly Victoria Terminus) and Dadar, that connect Mumbai to all the major cities and towns of India.

Railway Enquiry
Ph 131, 132, 134, 135

Porters: All stations have a licensed porter facility. They sport a metal armband with a number on it. It is advisable to use the services of a licensed porter or coolie, and to note the number on his armband, since they tend to move rapidly and you may lose them with your luggage in the crowd.

For the latest information on train schedules, booking status log on to:
www.indianrail.gov.in

For booking tickets on the internet log on to:
www.irctc.com

Indrail Passes: Indrail Passes for travel in India by train can be booked in India or abroad. The fares of Indrail Passes are given in US Dollars and payments can only be made in foreign currency.

Foreign nationals and non-resident Indians may buy railway tickets against payment in US dollars. Such tickets get a priority on reservation under the Foreign Tourist Quota and are exempt from reservation fee.

Local Transport

For travelling within the city you can engage a local taxi, easily available at all hotels and taxi stands. Taxis and autorickshaws in smaller cities are not metered and it is best to fix the rate beforehand, and to bargain.

Autorickshaws: A three-wheeled, black-and-yellow canopied contraption, an autorickshaw carries up to three passengers at a time, and is a cheap way to travel from point to point.

Cyclerickshaws: Cyclerickshaws are a common sight in most parts of urban and rural India. They are a convenient means of covering short distances. Not only do they precariously balance two to three people, they often carry merchandise as well.

Buses: Extensive bus networks connect most of India, in fact buses are one of the cheapest, most frequent and at times even the fastest mode of transport when travelling short distances.

STD CODES

Aurangabad	0240
Ajanta	02438
Ellora	02437
Fardapur	02438
Jalgaon	0257
Nasik	0253

Car Rentals: There are several international and local companies that operate car rental services in major Indian cities. Most car rentals accept international credit cards.

Tips or *Baksheesh*

Courtesy demands that you tip a waiter in a restaurant or hotel. The general norm is to pay 10% of the billed amount. Taxis, autorickshaws, public transport staff, government officials, or private service providers are not expected to be tipped. It is entirely up to you to tip someone for services rendered.

INTERNATIONAL AIRLINES OFFICES IN DELHI AND MUMBAI

Air India
Jeevan Bharati Bldg
124 Connaught Circus
Ph 011-23731225
Airport Ph 011-25653132
Mumbai Ph 022-26265555

Aeroflot
15/17 Tolstoy House
Tolstoy Marg
Connaught Place
Ph 011-23723241,
23310426
Airport 011-25653510
Mumbai
Ph 022-22821476/1682

Air Canada
Alps Building, 1st Floor
56 Janpath, Connaught Place
Ph 011-23720014
Airport
Ph 011-25656431/6421
Mumbai
Ph 022-23643299

Air France
7 Atma Ram Mansion
Scindia House
Ph 011-23738004,
23312853, 23310068,
23310069
Airport Ph 011-25652294
Mumbai Ph 022-22024818

Air Lanka
G-55 Connaught Place
Ph 011-23731473/1474,
23711334
Airport Ph 011-25652957,
25654733
Mumbai Ph 022-22844148,
22836065

Alitalia
Airport Ph 011-25652621

American Airlines
C-38 Connaught Place
Ph 011-23415284,
23411994
Mumbai Ph 022-22824467

Austrian Airlines
Himalaya House, 1st Floor
KG Marg, Connaught Place
Ph 011-23350113
Airport Ph 022-25654222

British Airways
DLF Plaza Tower
DLF Qutub Enclave
Phase-I, Gurgaon, Haryana
Ph 95124-5120747
Airport Ph 011-25652908,
25652078
Mumbai Ph 022-22820888,
22852904

Cathay Pacific
107-110 Kanchenjunga Bldg,
1st Floor
18 Barakhamba Road,
Connaught Place
Ph 011-23323332,
23325789
Airport Ph 011-25654701
Mumbai Ph 022-56572222

Druk Air
Ansal Bhawan, Room No.3
Ground Floor, 16 KG Marg
Ph 011-23357703/7704
Airport Ph 011-25653207

Emirates
DLF Centre, 7th Floor
Parliament Street
Connaught Place
Ph 011-55314444
Mumbai Ph 022-28797979

Gulf Air
G-12, Marina Hotel
Outer Circle
Connaught Place
Ph 011-23327814,
23324293
Airport Ph 011-25652065
Mumbai Ph 022-22024065

Japan Airlines
Chandralok Bldg
36 Janpath
Ph 011-23327104,
23327108
Ph 011-25653941
Mumbai Ph 022-22833136

KLM
Prakash Deep Bldg
7 Tolstoy Marg
Ph 011-23357747,
23357757
Airport Ph 011-25652715
Mumbai Ph 022-26828607

Korean Air
303-304 Prakash Deep Bldg
7 Tolstoy Marg
Ph 011-23721913/1914
Airport Ph 011-25654113
Mumbai Ph 022-22001946,
22088910

Lufthansa
56 Janpath
Ph 011-23724200
Airport Ph 011-25652064
Mumbai Ph 022-56301933

Royal Jordanian
G-56 Connaught Place
Ph 011-23327418
Airport Ph 011-25652478
Mumbai Ph 022-22022779

Royal Nepal Airlines
44 Janpath
Ph 011-23722989,
23321164
Airport Ph 011-25696876
Mumbai Ph 022-23321572,
23320817

SAS
Ambadeep Bldg, 6th Floor
14 KG Marg
Ph 011-23738789,
23352299

Singapore Airlines
9th Floor, Ashoka Estate
Barakhamba Road
Ph 011-23356286
Airport Ph 011-25653072
Mumbai Ph 022-22022747

Thai
Hotel Park Royal
1st Floor, Nehru Place
Ph 011-51497777
Airport Ph 011-25652413
Mumbai Ph 022-56373737

Turkmenistan Airways
N-1 BMC House
Middle Circus
Connaught Place
Ph 011-23721085,
23318247
Airport Ph 011-25654437,
2331004438
Mumbai Ph 022-2285107

PHRASE BOOK

In Emergency

English	Hindi	Marathi
Help!	*Bachao!*	*Madat kara!*
Stop!	*Rukho!*	*Thamba!*
Medicines	*Davai*	*Aushadh*

Please call a doctor/ambulance
H *Doctor/ambulance ko bulaiye*
M *Doctor kimwa ambulance bolwa*

Where is the nearest hospital?
H *Nazdeek hospital kahan hain?*
M *Jawal hospital kuthe aahe?*

I'm not feeling well
H *Meri tabiyat theek nahin hai*
M *Mazi tabyet theek nahi*

Where is... ?
H *Kahan hai...?*
M *Kuthe aahe?*

When will... be back?
H *Vaapas kab ayenge?*
M *Parat kadhi yenar?*

Call the police
H *Police ko bulaiye*
M *Police bolwa*

Useful Words

English	Hindi	Marathi
hot	*garam*	*garam*
cold	*thanda*	*thanda*
good	*achcha*	*changle*
bad	*bura*	*waieet*
open	*khula*	*ughade*
close	*bandh*	*bund*
left	*baayen*	*dawikade*
right	*daayen*	*ujwikade*
near	*paas*	*jawal*
far	*dur*	*laamb*
up	*oopar*	*warti*
down	*neeche*	*khali*
outside	*bahar*	*baaher*
inside	*andar*	*aat*
fast	*jaldi*	*lavkar*
slow	*dheere*	*haloo*
car	*gadi*	*motar*
bus	*bus*	*bus*
road	*sarak*	*rasta*
way	*raasta*	*waat*
house	*ghar/makaan*	*ghar*
door	*darwaaza*	*darwaaza*
fan	*pankha*	*pankha*
electricity	*bijlee*	*weej*
train	*train, rail gadi*	*train*
aeroplane	*hawai jahaj*	*viman*

Shopping

What is this?
H *Yeh kya hain?*
M *Hey kaay ahe?*

Do you have change?
H *Khule paise milenge?*
M *Sute paise miltil?*

Do you have...
H *Aap ke paas...hain?*
M *Aaplya kade...aahet?*

How much does this cost?
H *Yeh kitne ka hai?*
M *Hyachi kimmat kiti aahe kaay?*

BIBLIOGRAPHY

Aall, Ingrid, 'Ajanta: An Appreciation', in A Ghosh (ed.), *Ajanta Murals* (Delhi, 1967).

Brown, Percy, *Indian Architecture, Buddhist and Hindu* (Mumbai, 1942).

Currim, Mumtaz and Michell George (eds.), *Dargahs: Abodes of the Saints* (Mumbai, 2004)

Ghosh, A (ed.), *Ajanta Murals* (New Delhi, 1967).

Gupte, R S, *The Iconography of the Buddhist Sculptures of Ellora* (Aurangabad, 1964)

Lady Herringham, *Ajanta Frescoes* (New Delhi, 1998).

Maharashtra Tourism Development Corporation, Ltd., *In and Around Ajanta and Ellora* (Mumbai, 1993).

Meshram, Pradip Shaligram, *Early Caves of Maharashtra – A Cultural Study* (New Delhi, 1991).

Useful Phrases

What is your name?
H *Aap ka naam kya hain?*
M *Aaple naav kaay?*

My name is...
H *Mera naam... hain*
M *Maze naav... aahe*

See you
H *Phir milenge*
M *Punha bhetuya*

What is the time?
H *Kitna baja hai?*
M *Kiti wajle?*

Where are you from?
H *Aap kahan se aaye hain?*
M *Aapan kuthun aalaat?*

Do you speak English?
H *Kya aap angreji bolte hain?*
M *Aapan ingrajji bolta ka?*

I don't understand
H *Maine nahin samjha*
M *Mala samajle nahi*

Please speak slow
H *Aap dheere-dheere boliye*
M *Aapan savkash bola*

Communication Essentials

English	Hindi	Marathi
greetings	*namaste/ namaskar*	*namaskar*
yes	*han*	*ho*
no	*nahin*	*nahi*
thank you	*dhanyavad/ shukriyan*	*dhanyavad*
money	*paisa/rupaye*	*paise/rupaye*
time	*samay*	*wel*
day	*din*	*diwas*
night	*raat*	*ratra*
morning	*subah*	*sakal*
evening	*shaam*	*sandhyakal*
afternoon	*dopeher*	*dupar*
today	*aaj*	*aaj*
tomorrow	*kal*	*udya*
yesterday	*kal*	*kaal*
food	*khana*	*jewan*
water	*paani*	*paani*
girl	*ladki*	*mulgi*
boy	*ladka*	*mulga*
woman	*aurat*	*baai/stree*
man	*aadmi*	*purush*
one/two	*ek/do*	*ek/don*
clothes	*kapda*	*kapde*
shoes	*joota*	*chappal*
big	*bara*	*motha*
small	*chhota*	*lahan*

Michell, George, *The Penguin Guide to the Monuments of India: Buddhist, Jain, Hindu* (London, 1990).

Mitra, Debala, *Ajanta* (Delhi, 1996, Reprint).

Mitra, Swati (ed.), *Speaking Stones: World Cultural Heritage Sites in India* (New Delhi, 2001).

Mitter, Partha, *Much Maligned Monsters: A History of European Reactions to Indian Art* (Chicago, 1992).

Nagaraju S, *Buddhist Architecture of Western India*, 250 BC-AD 300 (Delhi, 1981).

Parimoo, Ratan *et al* (eds.), *The Art of Ajanta: New Perspectives* (New Delhi, 1991).

Plunkett, Richard *et al* (eds.), *Lonely Planet South India* (Melbourne, 2001).

Rowland, Benjamin, *The Art and Architecture of India: Buddhist, Hindu, Jain* (New York, 1977, Reprint).

Singh, Madanjeet, *The Cave Paintings of Ajanta* (London, 1965).

ARRIVING IN AURANGABAD

For centuries, Khirki, a dusty little village in the Marathwada region, was the gateway through which scores of conquerors and travellers from the north gained access to the south. The settlement was probably established during the Satvahana period (200 BC), however, it was the Mughal emperor Aurangzeb, who built walls around the settlement, and named it Aurangabad. The city, strategically important for the emperor in his expansionist policy in southern India, soon became a thriving centre of trade and commerce. Its textiles became much sought after, and even today the weavers of this region produce fine textiles like Paithani, Himroo and Kimkhwab.

Connected to major cities in India by air, rail and road, Aurangabad provides easy access to major Buddhist, Jaina, and Muslim monuments around it.

Ellora-Aurangabad Festival

The annual Ellora-Aurangabad Festival of Classical Dance and Music is held in December for three days in the campus of the Dr Baba Saheb Ambedkar Marathwada University. An arts and crafts fair is also held at the same time to highlight the rich cultural heritage, handicrafts, and handlooms of the region.

Bibi-ka-Maqbara and Panchakki are the two historical monuments in Aurangabad that are a must for tourists.

Panchakki is an amazing 17th century water mill, designed by Malik Ambar to generate energy to turn large stones that ground grain. A mosque and a series of dancing water fountains in the inner enclosure are the other attractions here.

Today, Aurangabad is a bustling city with a strong industrial presence. Major industrial houses like Bajaj Auto, Garware and Videocon have set up industries on its outskirts. The city boasts of many educational institutions, the most famous being the Dr Babasaheb Ambedkar Marathwada University.

The southern part of Aurangabad has the railway station and tourist offices. The bus stand is 1.5 kms further north. The more expensive restaurants and hotels are clustered along Jalna Road. To reach the World Heritage sites of Ajanta and Ellora, a visitor can choose between taxis and state transport buses that run to and fro from the sites.

Arriving by Air

The Chikkalthana Airport, approximately 10 kms from the city can be reached by hiring a taxi, which will cost around Rs 120. Daily flights operated by Indian Airlines and Jet Airways link Aurangabad to New Delhi and Mumbai.

Airline Offices

Indian Airlines
Airport Road
Ph 0240-2483390/5421
Fax 0240-2485012
Airport Ph 0240-2485780
Fax 0240-2482111

Jet Airways
4 Vidya Nagar, Jalna Road
Ph 0240-2441770/1392/5421
Airport Ph 0240-2487076/4269/

Flight no.	Delhi-Aurangabad-Delhi
IC 887/888	**Daily**

Flight no.	Mumbai-Aurangabad-Mumbai
9W3103/3104	**Daily**
IC887/888	**Daily**
9W3109/3110	**Daily**

Arriving by Train

Aurangabad is well connected to Mumbai by train. However, for the traveller coming from Delhi the options by train to Aurangabad are few. Jalgaon, 161 kms away, on the Central Railway mainline, is much better connected.

Railway Enquiry
Ph 131/2333966
Ticket Status 132

Arriving by Road

Aurangabad is connected by road to most major cities in Maharashtra, Mumbai, Pune, Shirdi and Nasik. Overnight buses leave Mumbai Central Bus Stand (Ph 022-23074272) every evening for Aurangabad.

Local Travel

Aurangabad is well connected by road to Ajanta, Ellora, Jalgaon and Daulatabad as well as Paithan, Lonar Crater, Khuldabad and Grishneshwar. Several state transport buses leave the Central Bus Stand for the above sites daily. The other option is to hire a car, which will cost approximately Rs 800 (non-air-conditioned) for the whole day. You can also hire an autorickshaw from the bus stand, which will take you to Daulatabad and Ellora Caves, though insist on going by the meter. For the enthusiastic traveller wishing to explore the city of Aurangabad, bicycles are available for hire near the Railway Station and Central Bus Stand.

Distances from Aurangabad

To	Kms
Ajanta	106 kms
Daulatabad	13 kms
Ellora	30 kms
Grishneshwar	30 kms
Jalgaon	161 kms
Khuldabad	26 kms
Lonar	145 kms
Mumbai	389 kms
Paithan	56 kms
Pithalkhora	78 kms
Pune	226 kms
Shirdi	136 kms

New Delhi - Aurangabad - New Delhi

Train Name	Train No	Frequency
Sachkand Super Express	2715/2716	Daily

New Delhi - Jalgaon - New Delhi

Train Name	Train No	Frequency
Jhelum Express	1077/1078	Daily
Punjab Mail	2137/2138	Daily
Karnataka Express	2627/2628	Daily

Mumbai - Aurangabad - Mumbai

Train Name	Train No	Frequency
Devagiri Express	1003/1004	Daily
Mumbai-Latur Express	1005/1006	Tue/Thu/Sat
Nandigram Express	7605/7606	Daily

Mumbai - Jalgaon - Mumbai

Train Name	Train No	Frequency
Dadar-Amritsar Express	1057/1058	Daily
Howrah-Bombay Mail	2809/2810	Daily
Vidarbha Express	2105/2106	Daily

Tours and guides

Maharashtra Tourism Development Corporation (MTDC) operates conducted tours from Mumbai to Aurangabad. In Aurangabad, MTDC operates daily sightseeing tours from the Central Bus Stand to Ajanta (0730-1730), Ellora and within Aurangabad (0800-1630). Conducted tours also leave from Holiday Resort on Station Road for Ajanta (0800-1730), Ellora and City (0930-1730). The tour of Ellora also includes a visit to major sites of Aurangabad like Daulatabad Fort, Aurangzeb's Tomb at Khuldabad, Bibi-ka-Maqbara, and Panchakki.

Central Bus Stand
Aurangabad Ph 0240-2331647

Where to Stay

Luxury

Taj Residency
8-N-12, CIDCO
Ph 0240-2381106/1107
Website: tajhotels.com

Rama International
R-3, Chikkalthana
Ph 0240-2485441/5442
Website: welcomhotelrama.com

Ambassador Ajanta
Jalna Road
CIDCO
Ph 0240-2485211/5212
Website: ambassadorindia.com

President Park
R-7/2, Chikkalthana
Airport Road
Ph 0240-2486201/6202

Quality Inn The Meadows
Village Mitmita
Dhule-Mumbai Road
Ph 0240-2677412,
2677413
E-mail: meadows@agd2.dot.net.in

Moderate

Aurangabad Ashok
Adalat Road
Ph 2332491/2493
Website: theashokgroup.com

Holiday Resort (MTDC)
Station Road
Holiday Camp
Ph 0240-2331513

Khemi's Inn
11 Town Centre
CIDCO
Ph 0240-2484868
E-mail: khemis@vsnl.com

Amarpreet
Pandit Nehru Marg
Jalna Road
Ph 0240-2332522
Website: amarpreethotel.com

Budget

YHA Hostel
Station Road West
Ph 0240-2334892

Tourist's Home
Station Road West
Ph 0240-2337212

Panchavati
Padampura Road
Ph 0240-2328755

Ajinkya
Nehru Place
Ph 0240-2335601

Where to Eat

Though eating out is not a very popular practice with the typical Aurangabadi, a visitor to the city need not despair since a variety of restaurants and fast-food joints catering to multiple tastes dot the city. The choice is varied depending on the budget; there are upmarket restaurants in 5-Star hotels or the reasonable Food Lovers on Station Road which serves good Punjabi and Chinese food. One of Aurangabad's most popular restaurants is Angeethi on Jalna Road, but if its real authentic Indian fare you're looking for, head to Thaliwala's Bhoj. Mingling on Jalna Road and Tandoor on Station Road are known for their tasty fare; budget restaurants along Station Road like Tirupati and Bharthi specialise in cheap south Indian meals. Bageecha on the Mumbai-Aurangabad highway with sprawling lawns is popular with travellers.

Shopping

Aurangabad is famous for its woven Himroo shawls, Mashru and Kimkhwab weaves, and the gorgeous Paithani *saris*. A wide range of semi-precious stones, agate in particular, is available in rough, polished and jewellery form. Bidriware or silver–embossed objects are also popular. The Paithani Silk Weaving Centre, opposite MGM College is very popular. The main shopping areas of Aurangabad are City Chowk, Gulmandi, Nawabpura, Shahganj, Sarafa and Mondha.

Paithan

Paithan, the ancient Pratishthana, is located 56 kms from Aurangabad on the banks of the river Godavari. Pratishthana, as the capital of the Satvahana dynasty, finds mention in the 1st century AD travelogue, *Periplus of the Erythraean Sea*. The shrine of Eknath Maharaj makes Paithan an important destination for Hindu pilgrims. An annual ten-day fair, the Paithan Yatra, is held in March/April.

Lonar Crater

Lonar, 145 kms from Aurangabad in Buldhana district, has one of the five largest meteorite craters in the world. It is conjectured that a high-velocity meteorite hitting the earth over 50,000 years ago caused the crater. Subsequently, a salt-water lake has formed within the depression.

The area around the crater is extremely fertile giving birth to a rich eco-system. The *Ain-i-Akbari* mentions that during Emperor Akbar's time there was a salt factory here. It is said that some of the best *beens* (musical instrument used by Indian snake charmers) are made of gourds growing in the area. The region is a veritable bird-watcher's paradise as a large number of migratory birds visit the place every winter.

Contact:

MTDC
Ph 07262-22026713/22024627
Buldhana Forest Officer
Ph 07262-242307, Fax 07262-243468.

Paithani *Saris*

Greek records of Ist century AD mention the gorgeous silken fabric made in Pratishthana. Famous for their vibrant colours and exclusive designs, Paithani *saris* come in pure silk, with elaborate *zari* work. The saris are named after the exquisite motifs woven on the borders and *pallavs* of the *sari*, for example, *tota-maina* will have parrots, *bangdi-mor* will have peacocks, while *asavali* have flowers and vines on it. Most of the *saris* are extremely intricate and can take between two months to two years to weave, depending on the design and therefore cost anything between Rs 6,000 to Rs 5,00,000.

Important Tourist Offices

Maharashtra Tourism Development Corporation (MTDC)
Head Office
Maharashtra Tourism Development Corporation
9th Floor, Express Towers, Nariman Point, Mumbai
Ph 022-22024482/ 22024522/22024584
Fax 022-22024521

Govt. of India Tourist Office
Krishna Vilas, Station Road, Aurangabad
Ph 0240-2364999, 2331217
Fax 0240-2331217
e-mail gitoaur@vsnl.com or indiatourism@agd2.net.in
Website www.tourismindia.com

Main reservation office
CDC Hutments, Opp. L.I.C. Building
Madame Cama Road, Mumbai
Ph 022-22026713/ 7762
Fax 022-22852182

MTDC Regional Offices

New Delhi
Maharashtra Information Centre
A/8 State Emporia Bldg
Baba Kharak Singh Marg
Ph 011-23363773

Aurangabad
Holiday Resort, Station Road
Ph 0240-2331513
Fax 0240-2331198

Pune
Central Building, I-Block
Ph 020-6126867/8169
Fax 020-6119434

Nagpur
Sanskritik Bachat Bhavan
Sitabuldi
Ph 0712-2533325
Fax 0712-2560680

Nasik
T/1 Golf Club, Old Agra Road
Ph 0253-2570059
Fax 0253-2579352

Amravati
C/o. B & C Rest House
Maltekdi Road
Telefax 0721-2674008

Ratnagiri
Collector Office Compound
Near Jaistambha
Telefax 02352-223847

Sindhudurg
New Administrative Building
C Block, 1st Floor
Telefax 02362-228785

Authorised Travel Agents of MTDC

Vaishali Tours & Travels (MTDC)
20 Dilli Haat, New Delhi
Ph 011-24672655, 24635464

Classic Travels
Aurangabad
Ph 0240-2335598/7788

Hospitals

Dhanwantari Hospital
Shriniketan Colony
Opp. Cosmos Bank, Jalna Road
Ph 0240-2334760

Govt. Medical College
Near Jubilee Park
Ph 0240-2402412/2413

Hedgewar Hospital
Near Trimurti Chowk, Garkheda
Ph 0240-2331994/1995

Post Office

June Bazar, Near Badkal Gate

Deccan Odyssey

Maharashtra Tourism runs a luxury train, Deccan Odyssey, on the lines of the Palace on Wheels. The train starts from Mumbai and also culminates there, in between it travels to several tourist destinations in Maharashtra and Goa. On reaching Aurangabad passengers are taken sight-seeing to Ajanta and Ellora caves. The total train journey is for a week and the train leaves Mumbai every Wednesday. For fares and other details you can log onto the following e-mail address or contact the telephone numbers mentioned below.

Half fare will be charged for children between 5 and 12 years of age.

India Marketing & Reservation Office:
Lawrence Travels & Tours (P) Ltd.
Ground Floor, Chandralok Builiding,
Janpath, New Delhi
Ph 011-23325939/3628, 23353155
Fax 011-23357478
E-mail: lawrence3@vsnl.com / info@deccanodyssey.com

Contact : Mr. Anil Zadoo
Mobile 00-91-98104-11414
Mr. Rajiv Varma
Mobile 00-91-98101-45718

USA Marketing & Reservation Office
357, West South Street
Carlisle PA-17013, USA
Telefax: (717) 240-0372
E- Mail: usa@deccanodyssey.com

ARRIVING IN AJANTA AND ELLORA

Ajanta

The drive from Aurangabad to Ajanta takes around two hours. Visitors have to disembark at the T-Junction in Fardapur (4 kms from the caves), and board the eco-friendly buses run by Maharashtra Tourism. The more adventurous could get off at Viewpoint (the place from where Captain John Smith first espied the caves), which is reached via a turnoff a short distance before the T-Junction. The view of the entire group of caves from here is stunning. From Viewpoint one may trek down the hilly path and eventually cross the footbridge that spans Waghora to reach the caves. In case you are taking the second option, arrange for your transport to collect you from the Fardapur parking lot after you finish sightseeing.

Staying in Ajanta

Ajanta provides only basic accommodation, but for those determined to stay here the following options are available.

MTDC Holiday Resort
Fardapur
Ph 02438-244230

Ajanta Travellers' Lodge
Near Ajanta caves
Ph 02438-244226

Fardapur Ext Resort
Kanhaiya Kunj
Ph 02438-244289

For bookings contact:

Aurangabad MTDC
Holiday Resort, Station Road
Ph 0240-2026713/4627

Govt of India Tourist Office
Krishna Vilas, Station Road
Aurangabad
Ph 0240-281217

Important Information

Guides are available at the ticket counter at both Ajanta and Ellora. You could also make prior bookings through the Superintending Archaeologist, ASI, Aurangabad Circle.

Timings

9.00 am to 5.30 pm
(Closed on Mondays and national holidays)

Entry Fee

For Indians above 15 years – Rs 10/-
For Others above 15 years – US $5 or Rs 250
Still photography (without flash) is free.

Special permission is required from the Archaeological Survey of India (ASI) to use tripods. However, video shooting from the exterior of the monuments is permitted on payment of a nominal fee of Rs 25.

For permission contact:

ASI, Janpath
New Delhi - 110011
Ph 011-23013574

ASI, Aurangabad Circle
Bibi-ka-Maqbara
Aurangabad - 431004
Ph 0240-2400620
Fax 0240-2400009

Ellora

Though the Ellora caves are just 30 kms from Aurangabad, you could hire a car for the day since the caves are spread out, and Daulatabad, Khuldabad and Grishneshwar may be made part of the trip.

Staying in Ellora

MTDC Kailas Hotel
Just facing the Ellora caves
Ph 02437-244543, 244446
E-mail hotelkailas.com

GLOSSARY

apsara	celestial nymph
Avalokitesvara	the Mahayana Bodhisattva of compassion
bhikshu	literally, a beggar; the name by which Buddha called his followers; a Buddhist monk is called *bhikshu*.
Bodhi	enlightenment, realisation. The *pipal* tree (*ficus religiosia*) came to be known as *Bodhi* tree after Buddha attained Enlightenment under the tree at Bodh Gaya.
Bodhisattva	the ideal of Mahayana tradition
chaitya	a sacred place; most commonly used as halls of worship
chhatra	the umbrella on top of the stupa; a traditional honorific symbol
chaitya-griha	a sanctuary of any kind; a Buddhist temple
chaitya-window	horseshoe-shaped window
chakra	literally, a wheel; a recurring motif in Buddhist art; a symbol of Buddha's teaching
chamara	fly whisk-bearer
chhatravali	triple umbrella on top of a stupa
dharma	translated variously as the natural law, the truth, the teaching of enlightened ones; refers to the teachings of Buddha
dharma-chakra	the wheel of law
gana	dwarf
gandharva	divine musician
hamsa	goose
harmika	the finial of a stupa in the form of a pedestal in which the shaft of the honorific umbrella was set
Hinayana	the lesser vehicle, referred to as such by practitioners of the Later Mahayana tradition, because the followers of the older Hinayana school aspired for individual enlightenment
Jatakas	the 547 *Jatakas* or Birth Stories are allegorical tales relating to Buddha's previous births
karuna	compassion
mahaparinirvana	the final extinction from *samsara*, the cycle of birth, life and death
Mahayana	literally, the great vehicle; the later school in Buddhism
Mara	the personification of evil; the temptor in Buddhist mythology who tried unsuccessfully to distract Buddha in his meditation
mriga	deer
mudra	gestures of the hand, each of which has a meaning; for example, *bhumisparsa-mudra* meaning touching the earth
naga	serpent demi-god, living in the netherworld
rakshasi	ogress
Rangit Leni	painted caves; local name for Ajanta caves
sala-bhanjika	tree nymph; motif representing a beautiful young woman
sangha	Buddhist community of monks and nuns, founded by Buddha in Sarnath
sangharama	Buddhist monastery
stupa	a dome-shaped Buddhist reliquary
torana	an arched entrance
tirthankara	preceptors in the Jaina religion. Mahavira was the twenty-fourth in the lineage of *tirthankaras*
vajra	thunderbolt
vajrasana	diamond seat
varshavasa	*varsha* means the rainy season and *vasa* means residence. *Varshavasa* means a rain retreat for the *sangha*
vihara	Buddhist monastery, generally with a central court or hall off which open small residential cells, has a Buddha shrine at one end
yaksha	mythical beings of pre-Buddhist Indian origin associated with fertility cults; *yaksha* and its female form, *yakshi*